In All the West
No Place Like This

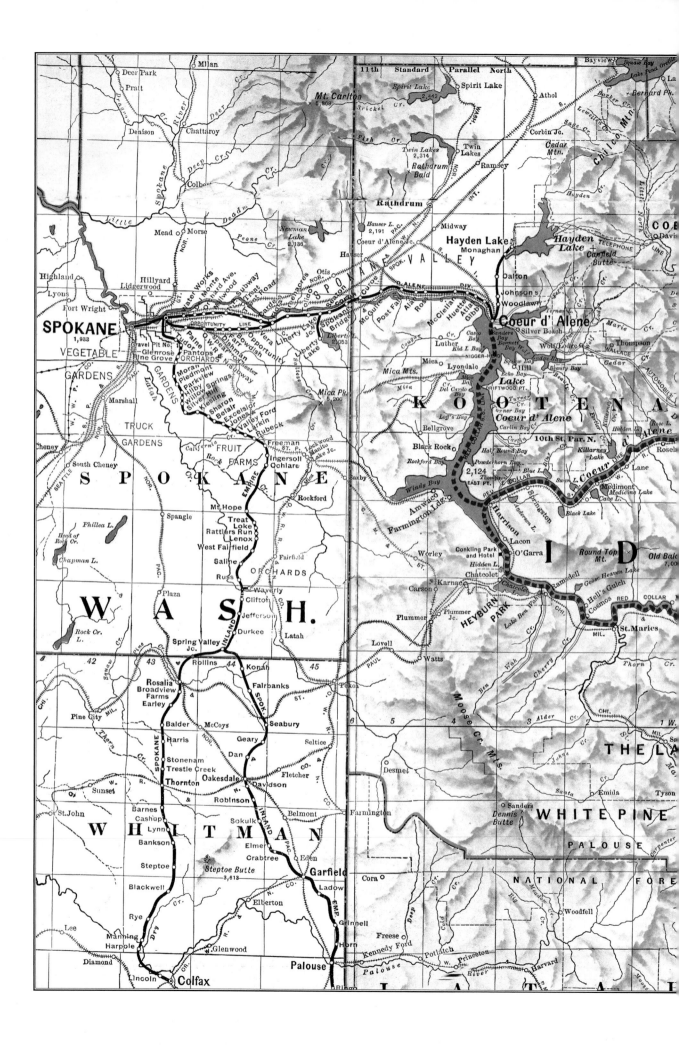

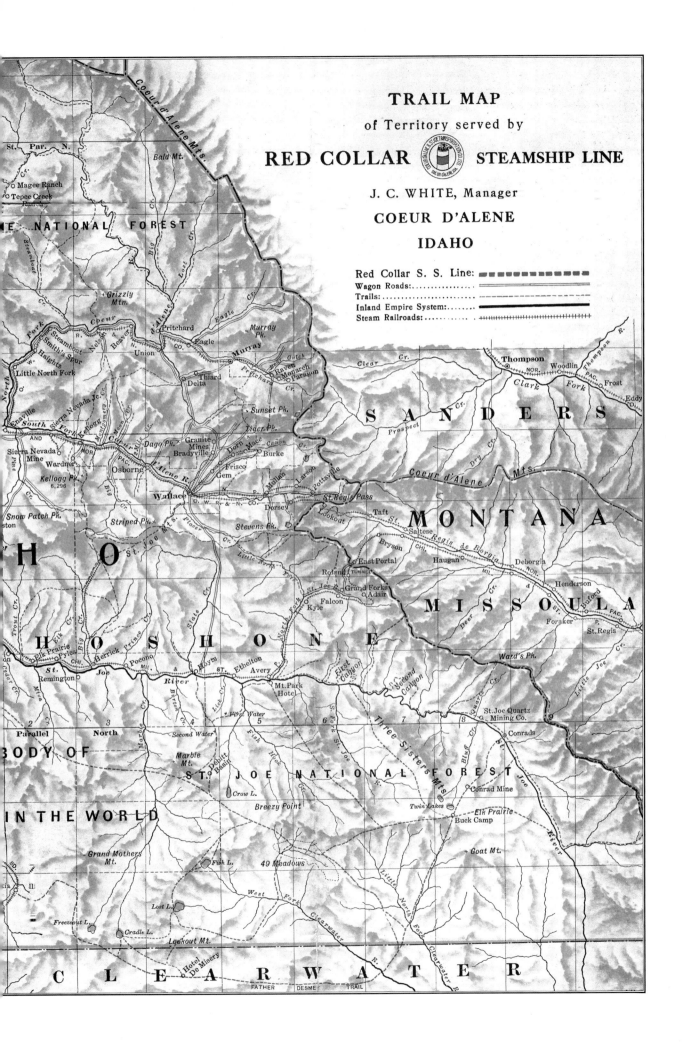

TRAIL MAP
of Territory served by
RED COLLAR STEAMSHIP LINE
J. C. WHITE, Manager
COEUR D'ALENE
IDAHO

Red Collar S. S. Line:	▬ ▬ ▬ ▬ ▬ ▬
Wagon Roads:	
Trails:	
Inland Empire System:	
Steam Railroads:	+++++++++++++++++++++

In All the West
No Place Like This

A Pictorial History of the
Coeur d'Alene Region

Revised

Dorothy Dahlgren
and
Simone Carbonneau Kincaid

Copyright 1996 Museum of North Idaho
PO Box 812
Coeur d'Alene, ID 83816-0812
(208) 664-3448
dd@museumni.org
www.museumni.org

Revised Edition 3rd printing 2009

Published by the Museum of North Idaho

CONTENTS

PREFACE

This book is the result of the Kootenai County Centennial Photograph Project, which began in 1988. Coordinator Simone Kincaid and volunteers took a quality copy camera to area communities. Residents brought their photograph collections in to be copied or donated their originals for preservation in the Museum of North Idaho. Over 500 photographs were copied and over 100 more were donated.

Dorothy Dahlgren and Simone Kincaid selected over 200 photographs for use in exhibits representing the area communities. These exhibit panels debuted at the Idaho Centennial kick-off during Fort Sherman Days in April 1990. Many people were interested in a book of the photographs so with the support of the Kootenai County Centennial Committee, the Museum of North Idaho, the Spokesman-Review/Spokane Chronicle, the North Idaho Community Action Agency and the Inland Empire Foundation, Dorothy and Simone added to the original project to create *In All The West No Place Like This: A Pictorial History of the Coeur d'Alene Region.*

The response to the first edition of *In All the West No Place Like This* was overwhelming, and the first printing sold out rapidly. Before going back to press, Dorothy and Simone searched for additional photographs to tell the story of the town of Harrison. The second edition included a chapter on Harrison and corrections of minor errors. This edition includes enhanced photographs, minor corrections and changes in the layout of the book.

ABOUT THE AUTHORS

Simone Carbonneau Kincaid graduated from Chico State University of California in 1977 with a B.A. in Anthropology and minors in Archaeology and Geology. She came to Idaho in 1976 and fell in love with the state. Since that time she has worked as an archaeologist for the University of Idaho, BLM, U.S. Forest Service and Northwest Archaeological Associates, Inc. Her major interests are historic mining, logging, Civilian Conservation Corps and Forest Service activities. In 1981 she coordinated the project to design and organize a catalogue system for the Museum of North Idaho's photograph collection. Simone is a local bookseller, archaeologist and continues to volunteer at the Museum of North Idaho.

Dorothy Dahlgren was born and raised in Coeur d'Alene, Idaho. She attended North Idaho College, then the University of Idaho where she graduated with a B.S. in Museology and History in 1982. She received a Masters in Organizational Leadership from Gonzaga University in 1998. Since 1982 she has been the curator of the photograph, archive and artifacts collections of the Museum of North Idaho as well as serving as the Director of the Museum.

MUSEUM OF NORTH IDAHO

The Museum of North Idaho, established in 1968, is a non-profit organization governed by a nine-member board of trustees. The museum's purpose is to preserve the history of the Coeur d'Alene region and to educate the public about that history. Membership is open to the public.

We are especially grateful to the people who had the foresight to save photographs, to take oral histories, to write about their own experiences, and to deposit these materials in museums and libraries for the benefit of the public. Without these people our local history would not be available. We wish to thank those who provided information for the project:

Felix Aripa
Centennial Newspaper Project
Sister Delores Ellwart, S.P.
Rose Goddard
Ed Healey
May and Jerry House
Lawrence Nicodemus
Robert Rickel
Wes Whiteman

Ed Brugger
Father Thomas Connolly, S.J.
Lavinia Felsman
Mr. and Mrs. John Harrison
Francis Heard
Kathryn McDaniel
Mildred Olsen
Marv Shadduck
Bob Worst

We also wish to thank those who worked on the project or donated materials:

Alice Allen
Betty Boykin
Barbara Chamberlain
Frame of Mind
Chris Gray
Terry Kincaid
Kay Grant Powers
Homer Schooler
Robert Singletary
Joe Turner
Al Wutzke

Atlas Building Supply
Camera Corral
Jan Edson
Jerry Gospodnetich
Warren Keating
North Idaho College
Pat Rollan
May Singleton
Connie Tremblay
Emma Weeks
Jim and Lee Yates

We extend our appreciation to the following people and organizations for allowing the Museum of North Idaho to copy their photographs, or for donating originals. Unfortunately not all of the photographs could be used in the book, but they are available for viewing at the Museum of North Idaho.

John Bacon
Edgar Benjamin
Bob Bishop
Herb Carlson
Bill Craner
Hans Dierks
Mr. and Mrs. Leroy Ellis
David Esterly
Carlene Frame
Laura Gaboury
Gordon Giles Estate
Lisa Goff
Virginia Hanks
Marianne Hensley
B.J. Hulteng
Peggy and Neil Irving
Margaret Jessick
Mary Lou Johnson
Ray Johnson
Kootenai County Extension Office
Jon Lafferty
Mrs. Marriman
Lois Carter Madley
Naomi Moen
David Osterberg
Carol Olsen
Margaret Shepperd
Post Falls Library
Mynard Rickard
Mrs. Frank Roth
Howard and Robert Rosenberry
Juanita and Barry Rust
Gladys Seiter
Elizabeth Shadwick
Priscilla Spain Spivey
Milton Stafford
U.S. Forest Service
Majorie Wadsworth
A.K. and Ellen Walden
Bertha Woolsey
Regina Zimmerman

Willav Beckman
Clyde Blake
Sadie Brooten
Crane Historical Society
Robert Conley
Loreen Ellersick
Keith Erickson
William Flatt
Mike Fritz
Lyn Galvin
Germaine Gregory
Mrs. Harold Hafterson
Catherine Hayes
Alex Holstein
Paul Hyde
Bette and Marlene Jacquet
Grace Johnson
P.W. Johnson Estate
Marvin Jones
Helen Knott
Bernice Larson
Florence Mead
Dee Moody
Montana State Historical Society
Old Mission State Park
Joy Porter
Post Falls Historical Society
Mary Rarick
Rose Lake Historical Society
Nortbert Rouleau
Lloyd Russell
Mrs. Sebring
Robert Sims
Spirit Lake Library
Georgia Smith
Gordon Streicher
Charles and Darlene Vedder
Marilyn Wagenius
Mildred Woolen
Amelia Yates

CIRCLING RAVEN: COEUR D'ALENE INDIANS

The Schee-Chu-Umsh: "the ones that were found here" were Sahlish-speaking people, who once occupied over 4 million acres in northern Idaho, Montana and eastern Washington. They were primarily a hunter-gatherer people who followed the seasonal cycle of wild game, fish runs, roots and berries. Extended families or one to three families lived in conical lodges constructed of poles and sewn tule mats. Villages and camps were primarily located on lakeshores or at special food gathering and processing locations.

The introduction of the horse by the Shoshone greatly altered the lifestyle of these people. After 1760 the Coeur d'Alene were able to hunt in the northern plains for buffalo until winter. Hides replaced grass mats and became the preferred material for carrying bags and housing. Transportation became easier with the use of travois pulled by horses.

Explorers and fur traders came into the Inland Northwest during the early 19th century and established trading posts among the Schee-Chu-Umsh people. David Thompson, of the Northwest Fur Trading Company, brought French-speaking Iroquois Indians with him as guides and scouts. These French-speaking Iroquois may have been the first to call the tribe the Coeur d'Alene. In his journals, Thompson referred to these Indians as "pointed hearts", which is probably a translation of the French words "Coeur d'Alene." An awl is a pointed tool used to pierce leather. Why the name was applied to the Schee-Chu-Umsh is uncertain, but the most widely accepted explanation is that it described their sharp trading practices.

Lewis and Clark recorded a meeting between traders and the Coeur d'Alene at a Nez Perce camp during the 1805 expedition. Contact with the trappers and traders not only brought trade goods that improved the Indian's life style but also brought disease, which reduced their number by eighty percent.

The Coeur d'Alene Chief, "Circling Raven", had a vision that one day men wearing black robes would bring spiritual power and teaching to his people. So when word of a missionary named Father DeSmet came to the Coeur d'Alene, by way of the Flathead Indians, they were eager to seek him out and learn the Catholic teachings. The Coeur d'Alene felt this black-robed priest was Circling Raven's vision come true. In the spring of 1842 the first meeting of the Coeur d'Alene and

Previous page: *The Cataldo Mission in a bad state of repair before its restoration.* Rel-2-19

the Black Robes occurred at the head of the Spokane River (the present site of North Idaho College) where they erected a log chapel and began teaching the natives. As an incentive for the natives to learn the numerous prayers the missionaries allowed them to smoke a pipe after they learned a commandment. The Coeur d'Alene referred to the Ten Commandments as the "Ten Pipes".

In the fall of 1844, the Coeur d'Alene went to St. Ignatius, Montana and brought two missionaries back to their people. These Black Robes established the first mission of the Sacred Heart at the mouth of the St. Joe River. This mission consisted of two log buildings but within two years the site had to be abandoned because of flooding. A new mission site was located along the banks of the Coeur d'Alene River on the knoll between the forest and the river. The Fathers and the Coeur d'Alene built the Cataldo Mission, which is the oldest standing building in Idaho. The Fathers taught the Coeur d'Alene agriculture and they grew hay, grains, and potatoes and maintained an orchard in an area of about one hundred acres.

The increased movement of settlers into the Northwest in the 1850s created distress and distrust among the Native Americans. By 1855, the U.S. Government, through Territorial Governor Stevens, began negotiating treaties with the various tribes in order to move the Indians onto reservations to allow for more settlement by the Euro-Americans. This lead to hostile retaliation by the natives including the murder of Yakima Indian Agent A.J. Bolan. Several conflicts and rumors of a military road convinced the Coeur d'Alene to join the Yakima, Spokane and Palus in a war against the U.S. Government. The Battle of Steptoe Butte and the retreat of Colonel Steptoe led to Colonel George Wright's campaign against the Spokane and Coeur d'Alene tribes. He demanded unconditional surrender from the Coeur d'Alene and Spokane tribes or promised total extermination. The destruction of the natives' beef cattle, granaries and eight hundred horses by Colonel Wright at the state line between Idaho and Washington brought an end to the conflict.

Father Joset from the Cataldo Mission convinced Colonel Wright that the Coeur d'Alene had helped Colonel Steptoe escape and therefore did not deserve retribution but rather fair treatment. Over the years, several treaties were made, each time reducing the tribe's land.

During the 1860s the Cataldo Mission became a supply point for prospectors traveling along the Mullan Road, which extended from Fort Benton, Montana to Fort Walla Walla, Washington. The increase in white settlers in the area created problems for the Coeur d'Alene and in 1877, the Jesuit Fathers encouraged the tribe to move south to their camas digging fields where vast farmlands were available for them to continue their successful farming practices. At the site of DeSmet, they established the third and the last Sacred Heart Mission.

DeSmet, about 1910. Named after Father DeSmet, this town included a three-story boys' boarding school, three-story girls' boarding school, rectory, Gothic church, Jesuit seminary building, and housing for the tribe.
Des-1-18

Gothic Church at DeSmet, built in 1885. A Coeur d'Alene named Old Agatha Timothy, one hundred years old or more, loved this church so much that she said she would take her beautiful church to heaven with her. On April 2, 1939, the day after she died, the church burned to the ground.
Rel-4-12

Interior of the Gothic church. The Catholic religion is an important aspect of the life of the Coeur d'Alene.
Rel-4-20

Sheep on the street at DeSmet, about 1910. The Coeur d'Alene raised sheep as well as other stock. Many of the Coeur d'Alene had large successful farms until 1909 when the government allotted each native only 160 acres, reducing the reservation by about one-third.
Agr-3-17

Coming into DeSmet. The people lived out on farms and only lived in the houses at DeSmet on weekends, religious holidays, and feast days.
Des-1-3

Indian Day at DeSmet, 1920s. On Indian Day the Indians would dress in native regalia and the children, both native and white, would dress up and perform plays. Standing, from left: Irene Rassmussen, Theresa Luke LaSarte, unknown. Sitting: Clotile Luke LaSarte and Regina Smith.
NA-1-11

New Year's well-wishers, January 1, 1918, at DeSmet. On January 1 the men put on masks and went around to all the houses wishing people a Happy New Year and shaking hands. More people would join them as they went to the next house.
NA-4-25

"When I was a kid, they would come into the house with masks on... I would get so scared that I would go behind my grandfather's chair and hide." —Lavinia Felsman

---

Coeur d'Alene Tribal Jail, 1910. Originally formed to help the church in its regular function, the "Soldiers of the Sacred Heart" became a tool of the Chief to bring drunks, adulterers, gamblers, and others to justice. The accused faced a panel of judges and often the penalties were severe. There were not many offenders, and as the members of the "Soldiers of the Sacred Heart" died out, they were not replaced.
Des-2-1

Eugene Sol Louie in his World War I uniform in DeSmet. The Coeur d'Alene went to war for the U.S. Government in WWI and WWII. When the men returned from WWII many of the families moved from the farms into DeSmet.
Des-1-2

The Coeur d'Alene Cubs Baseball Team, 1920. Baseball has long been a favorite sport among the Coeur d'Alene. They played teams from around the area. Top, from left: Slugger ToTo, Joe Vincent, Louie Aripa, Eugene Sol Louie, Joe Skanen. Bottom, from left: John Zachary, unknown, unknown, Nick SiJohn, Jack Zachary. Front: Louie Meshell and Amos Bachette.
NA-5-11

Procession at DeSmet, 1918. Large processions were held for the arrival of church dignitaries, such as this one for Bishop Gorman.
Rel-7-27

Father John Keep, 2nd from the left, standing by the Gothic Church, c. 1915.
Rel-6-22

Nuns at DeSmet working in the garden. The Sisters of Charity of Providence had a large garden at the mission where they grew food to feed themselves and the children at the school. Everything was canned and stored in the basement of the school and during the winter, they often gave food to those in need. *Rel-6-9*

Working in the kitchen. The Sister and the young woman are making a pie with fruit gathered from the orchards that surrounded the mission. *Rel-6-33*

Tall Timothy on the right. The Coeur d'Alene adopted European dress shortly after the arrival of the missionaries. They wore their native dress on holidays and special occasions.
NA-1-13

Coeur d'Alene Indians in native dress, c. 1910.
NA-1-9

Coeur d'Alene woman with her horse, c. 1915.
NA-6-54

NA-7-10

Coeur d'Alene woman and children at tepee. Tepees were used
as temporary shelters for hunting, social events and gathering
berries or camas. For centuries, camas was used by the Coeur
d'Alene. The root, which resembles an onion, is often boiled.
NA-7-10

Nancy and Clarence Prosper are shown here in native costume.
NA-1-31

"Several years ago all of a sudden we realized we're losing our language. We have it in school now. This is a great thing. I believe that if we can hold on to our language, we can hold on to our customs and keep up with some of the stories and some of the things our people did a long time ago. I believe it's really important to retain our language. If we can do that then our stories and our Indian thinking would remain with us. If we lose our language, we will lose everything. We won't be Indians anymore." —Lawrence Aripa

OPENING THE RESERVATION: WORLEY

In 1909, a million acres of farm and timberland in the Spokane, Coeur d'Alene and Flathead Indian Reservations were opened up for homesteading. The town sites of Plummer and Worley were established on the former reservation lands south of Coeur d'Alene.

Worley was platted in 1908 in anticipation of the opening of the reservation. Charles Worley was the first Indian Agent and the town was named for him.

Early homesteaders had to clear the land of timber before it was suitable for agriculture. Many made their living by making and selling hand-hewn railroad ties.

Overview of Worley, about 1920. The community church is in the foreground. It was built in 1916. Parsons livery barn is on the right. The Worley Hotel, the harness shop and Mottern's General Store are also visible.
Wor-1-3

Opposite page: ***The Chicago, Milwaukee, and St. Paul Railroad at Worley.*** The Milwaukee Railroad came through Worley in 1913. This provided transportation for agricultural and timber products to area markets.
TRR-5-32

Worley street scene. On the left is Walser's Store, left center is the post office, and on the right is the Svendsgaard Store.
Wor-1-1

Worley Post Office, 1932. Charles Hoag, foreground, postmaster of Worley. He served from 1914 to 1942. Cecil Acres and Roy Holt were rural mail carriers. The post office was established in 1911 and Zula Walsa was the first postmaster. *Wor-1-2*

Dedication of the Worley School, Spring 1915. Front row: Seventh child from the left is Jean Svendsgaard, boy behind sitting baby is Frank Lane, seventh from the right is Carl Parsons (boy). Second row: second from the left is Charles Hoag, then Mrs. Cronk, unknown girl, Mrs. Lane, first from the right with a mustache is Mr. Wilson, third from the right is Claude Hickman. *Wor-8-3*

Threshing scene, about 1915. After the reservation was reduced in size in 1909, the Coeur d'Alene could not afford the expensive machinery for wheat and hay farming and many had to lease their lands to the new settlers. *Agr-1-23*

THE LOWER COEUR D'ALENE RIVER VALLEY

The lower Coeur d'Alene River Valley was settled by a few homesteaders prior to the discovery of rich mineral deposits in the Coeur d'Alene Mining District. With the influx of miners into the area, others settled in the vicinity to supply agricultural products and lumber for the mining industry. The Coeur d'Alene River Valley was a fertile farming area but many of the farmers who settled the area had to clear the logs off the land before they could farm. They were known as "stump ranchers". Mills were built along the lower Coeur d'Alene River to process the logs.

In the late 1890s, the Oregon, Washington Railway and Navigation Company completed its line from Harrison through the Coeur d'Alene River Valley and into the Mining District. Many communities were established in the area. Medimont was settled in the 1890s in anticipation of great mineral findings in nearby mountains. By 1903 Lane had a population of one hundred, two general stores, a hotel, two churches and a school. By 1912 Rose Lake had surpassed Lane as the leading community with a population of two hundred, and by 1916 Rose Lake boasted five hundred residents.

The lower Coeur d'Alene River Valley is dotted with numerous small lakes, many known for their great fishing and recreation. Rose Lake even had a resort with a floating boardwalk.

Previous page: ***Hans Dierks homestead, Lane.*** This family homesteaded at Lane in the early 1900s growing grains and hay and raising cattle and horses.
He-1-9

A cabin in Latour Creek, after 1910. Allie Helman, Anna Hughes, George Hughes, and Calais Hughes. Many homesteads were located along Latour Creek and at one time there was a school at the mouth of the creek.
He-1-53

Artemus Cathcart's Band at Lane, 1907-1910. The band is in front of the Latimer Dance Hall. Lane, established in the 1880s was named after a local logger. First row left: Latimer (twins either Elisha or Lije), John Helm, Art Cathcart, Hans Dierks, William Dierks, and Clyde Quarles. Back row left: Latimer (twin), Ira Allen, Frank Seaman, Ray Quarles, Winchester, Ira Treefly, Bill Siebert.
RL-11-1

Threshing scene at the Triplet ranch, Rose Lake. Fort Sherman provided the first market for hay and grain from the Rose Lake-Cataldo area. Later the loggers, miners, and mills needed hay and grains for their horses. Elvier Oehrling, far right, is the owner of the machine.

Agr-1-2

Harvesting hay at Hans Dierks' homestead, Lane. This baling
operation involves men standing on the stack pitching loose
hay into the cylinder of the baler, which is at left center (the
end of one bale is showing). Horses go around and around, the
windlass drum tightens the cable, which pushes against the
hay, forming the bales, and each bale is weighed.
Agr-1-6

Oat Fields at Rose Lake, about 1910. Horses were used extensively during this time, requiring a great amount of hay and grain for feed.
Agr-5-1

Springston. First named Anderson, after a nearby lake, Springston was located up the Coeur d'Alene River three miles from Harrison. The first mill was built in 1901. When it burned in 1907, a new mill was built; then sold to Russell and Pugh and in 1958 the Russells bought out the Pughs. Operations continued until 1964 when the mill was dismantled. Springston was a stop on the Oregon, Washington Railway and Navigation line and served as a shipping point for lumber.
Sgn-1-3

Dwyer's store at Cataldo. The community of Cataldo, named after Father Cataldo, is located about a half-mile from the mission. *Cat-1-4*

The Canyon School, 1924. The teacher is India T. Hilslip. First row from left: Esther Sverdsten, unknown, Dorothy Beamis. Second row: end of the row is Mary Evelyn Smith. Third row, from left: unknown, Agnes Smith, Sadie Assad Brooten. Primarily stump ranchers settled the area around Canyon. *RL-8-13*

Rose Lake. The Rose Lake Post Office was established in 1905. Rose Lake is possibly a misspelling of the name of an early settler named Rows although another story is that it was named after Rose Brown, a homesteader on Rose Creek, and then known as Cougar Gulch. Rose Lake was primarily a company town whose economy was based on the logging and lumber industry; however, farming--prevalent in the area because of the fertile flood plain of the Coeur d'Alene River--contributed to the economy. The Oregon, Washington Railway and Navigation Company provided service to the town.
RL-1-1

Kellers Hall, about 1928. The ramp was built between the railroad and the building over the slough. This building was also used as the Odd Fellows Hall.
RL-4-1

The Winton Store. Leigh LeGore managed the store from 1911 to 1929. This company store contained a variety of merchandise including hardware, hay, wheat, dry goods, shoes, and groceries. The post office was also located in the store. The Winton Lumber camps and local residents were supplied from the store.
RL-1-2

The Rose Lake Service Station. Harvey Mutch and his tow truck, about 1922. This building was previously a saloon.
RL-3-1

The Rose Lake School. Built in 1913 by the Winton Lumber Company this school was used for first through eighth grades. High school students took the train to Harrison until the 1930s when high school classrooms were added. At this time another small building was added to accommodate first to third grades. The last high school class to graduate was in 1957 and the school closed in 1985.
RL-8-5

Rose Lake Football team. First row, from left: unknown, Ray Benum, Frank Snyder, Jack Gray, Ernie Conner, Virgil Earling, Ralph Snyder, Dave Healy, Jim Ryan. Second row, from left: Elmo Wilcox, Reese Hubbard, Lloyd Gilman, Bull (Vernon) Earling, Chic Bowen.
RL-8-11

Rose Lake during the flood of 1933. By December 1933 there was a
heavy snow pack. A Chinook wind began to blow and by Christmas
there was flooding throughout the Coeur d'Alene River area. The
bridge at Rose Lake was swept away almost killing seven boys.
Livestock was carried down river and considerable property damage
was done.
Mil-12-6

The bridge at Rose Lake, 1912. The 1917 flood washed out this
bridge, along with the bridges at Lane and Dudley. The Rose
Lake bridge was rebuilt with scrap iron from the bridge they
found down river after the flood.
Mil-12-27

The YMCA. This is the second YMCA built by the Rose Lake Lumber Company. The first burned in 1913. The YMCA building housed single men who worked for the mill. It had a theatre, three bowling alleys, and a gym. It was used for all kinds of community functions including church and Christmas gatherings, until it burned in about 1935.
RL-12-3

The cooks at the boarding house of the Rose Lake Lumber Company. Rose Lake Lumber Company Number Three included a large boarding house and YMCA building.
Mil-12-18

The Rose Lake Lumber Company and the burner. W.J. Johnson
operated the first Rose Lake Lumber Company at Lane, for A.W.
Crawford, until it was destroyed by fire in 1903. A new mill was
built three miles east from the old mill and began production in
1905. Crawford, Page and Devlin incorporated the second Rose Lake
Lumber Company in 1906 but this mill burned in 1909. In 1911 Rose
Lake Lumber Company Number 3 began operation, on a site further
east along the Coeur d'Alene River, under the control of Charles and
David Winton and Walter Rosenberry. Winton and Rosenberry oper-
ated the Rose Lake Lumber Company from 1911 to 1929.
Mil-12-4

The green chain at the Rose Lake Lumber Company. Lumber
production rose, then dipped and rose again in the 1920s.
At its highest point in 1926, the ten counties of North Idaho
produced 950,000,000 board feet of timber. In 1932, it would
dip to 200,000,000 board feet. Although production had
boomed in northern Idaho and the nation during the 1920s
wages were kept low. With the consequent drop in demand,
compared with production, came the depression. Between
1930 and 1933, nearly 50 percent of the woodworkers in
North Idaho were laid off.
Mil-12-13

Lumber cart at the Rose Lake Lumber Company. Horses were used here until the mill closed in 1929.
Mil-12-2

Row houses of the Rose Lake Lumber Company at Rose Lake.
Known as "The Row," these company houses were rented
to men who worked at the Rose Lake Lumber Company
mill. The company doctor and an occasional Forest Service
employee also stayed in these houses.
Mil-12-21

The Whiteman Lumber Company, 1936. Harry Whiteman
and his son Wes were lumbermen for more than 30 years.
They had sawmills and planers at three locations in the Rose
Lake area. From 1928 to 1988 they provided mine stull for the
Sunshine Mining Company.
Mil-7-24

The Winton and Rosenberry Lumber Camp, 1920s. The Winton
Lumber Company operated many camps like this one all along the
Little North Fork of the Coeur d'Alene River and along the tributaries
of the North Fork of the Coeur d'Alene River on national forest lands.
This camp is believed to be one of the five camps located along Falls
Creek.
Log-6-29

*Concerning the cook at Cathcart Creek camp, of the Winton Lumber Company. "...he would have
a little brew because the fruit was parched on the table, there was no juice in it. And, whenever
he got a rare of that when it get fermented and he got drinking it, why he took a butcher knife
and a cleaver and he cleaned up...there was usually, in the camp... you'd have two--a couple
of flunkeys, or three flunkeys... (depending on) the size of the camp...a dishwasher and a cook.
So, Terrible Tom would race through the cookhouse with a butcher knife and a cleaver and he'd
clean the cookhouse. You'd see 'em coming out of the windows and the doors and everyplace
else. So, that's how he got his name, Terrible Tom. And, had a walking boss there, old Bronc
McManamin... he'd fire old Terrible Tom and send him to town, and then they'd send another
cook in. Usually it's pretty hard to get a good camp cook, just off the records quick. Like, see
we had Featherstone, the employment agency in Spokane--they'd call C.V. Huck, order a cook
right away to replace Terrible Tom. And, this cook would come and probably he couldn't cook at
all, just be a 'belly burglar' as we used to call 'em. And, the crew would start to grumble so old
Bronc would fire him and hire another one. He'd be just as bad, so then, he'd call Featherstone
and C.V. Huck say, "Have you saw Terrible Tom in Town?" "Yes". "How's he look?" "He's
sobering up." "Send him up." So, Terrible Tom would come back. He'd go on another drunk and
the same thing would go over. And it went on that way for years."*
-Dooley Cramp

Forest Service officer Charles Larson scaling timber on the Skookum Creek Sale in the Coeur d'Alene National Forest, 1924. In the early years of the Forest Service rangers were primarily involved with checking homestead claims, construction and maintenance of fire lookouts and trails. The demand for white pine timber brought lumber companies onto federal lands, giving the Forest Service rangers the additional responsibility of administering timber sales. One of their duties included scaling logs (measuring logs to estimate board feet) taken from federal lands.
Log-1-9

Logging at the Skookum Creek sale. On the left a horse can be seen pulling logs down a chute where they are transferred to a roll away then into a flume that carried the logs to a holding area on the Coeur d'Alene River. The cost of the flume was $9,000 per mile. The Winton Lumber Company was one of many companies that participated in spring log drives in order to transport logs down river to the mills. The logs would be flumed down creeks to the river, then held in ponds behind a series of splash dams. When there were enough logs in the river and enough water behind the dams the dams would be opened, starting with the one farthest upstream. This began the log drive. Once the logs reached the main Coeur d'Alene River they were sorted at Dudley according to ownership brands stamped into the logs then towed to their respective mills. Those headed for Coeur d'Alene mills were sorted again at Harrison.
Log-1-10

Greasing the chute.
Log-1-7

"You just got a big ole five gallon can full of grease of some kind and a bunch of rags wrapped around a stick and you walk up the chutes-slip slop-you know, grease the chutes in the places were the logs are apt to slow down... When they start a trail of logs down there the guy lets a hoop out that logs are comin'. Others relay that down and get out of the way. I didn't hear the guy a holler. I heard a little noise and I looked up and here comes the logs I took a dive off that chute and I was sure glad I did, a whole bunch of 'em went off right there. Any kind of a job you do in the woods is dangerous. In those days there wasn't much recourse that a workin' man had, that I know of, maybe they'd pay for his funeral."
-Ed Cyr

The "Sorting Gap" at Dudley, about 1914. The logging railroad followed Fourth of July Creek to Dudley, where the logs were dumped
into the Coeur d'Alene River. Fire in Fourth of July Canyon in 1917
ended much of the logging.
Log-4-45

Winton and Rosenberry log drive crew near Cataldo, 1933. After the Rose Lake Lumber Company closed in 1929, logs were towed to the Winton and Rosenberry sawmill (later the site of Northwest Timber) at Gibbs, near Coeur d'Alene until 1946.
Log-4-49

Log jam on the Coeur d'Alene River. This log jam contained fifteen million feet of logs from the Breakwater Dam, two miles upriver. The logs were picked up by the flood-waters in 1933 and crammed into a half mile of river above Breakwater. It took five teams, twenty log drivers, a steam donkey and a bulldozer with drums, twenty-eight days to break them down while other log drivers kept them moving downriver.
Log-4-67

***Loading logs on the railroad at the Fourth of July Canyon,
Rose Lake Lumber Co.*** The Rose Lake Lumber Company
logged the Fourth of July Canyon area and the logs were
transported to Dudley, on the Coeur d'Alene River, where they
were towed by steamboat to the mill at Rose Lake.
Log-7-41

***Hoo Hoo Lumber Company shay engine at Rose Lake, 1906-
1909.*** The Hoo Hoo Lumber Company operating in the Rose
Lake area from 1906 to 1909. They ran a narrow gauge railroad
up Rose Creek.
Log-8-14

FROM WESTWOOD TO RATHDRUM

A hunter and trapper named Connors built a squatter's cabin in 1861, later used for a relay station by the Pony Express. Charles Wesly Wood eventually bought the rights to Conner's cabin and established a ranch on the land. This land became the town of Westwood. In 1881 a post office was established, but the government would not accept the name Westwood as there were too many towns by that name in the territory. A resident suggested the name of his native town in Ireland, Rathdrum. By 1881 the town was surveyed and platted by C.W. Wood and M.D. Wright and it held the position of County Seat for Kootenai County.

During the 1880s the town boomed as a supply point for the Coeur d'Alene Mining District. Rathdrum supported a variety of businesses including hotels, mercantiles, and a brewery. Frederick Post built a sawmill in Rathdrum and established a gravity water system from the Spring Branch Dam in 1883. In 1886 D.C. Corbin built a spur line from the Hauser Junction to Coeur d'Alene, which cut Rathdrum off as a supply point for the mining district. In spite of this, the removal of the county seat in 1908 and numerous fires, Rathdrum continued to maintain a certain level of prosperity.

The non-irrigated tracts of land near Rathdrum produced abundant crops of hay, cereals, fruits and vegetables. This area was also used to raise stock and poultry. As lands were logged off, agricultural lands were expanded and new irrigation systems were incorporated using nearby mountain lakes and streams. D.C. Corbin built an extensive system of irrigation ditches across the Rathdrum Prairie.

Opposite page: *Overview of Rathdrum, April 1887.* A Pony Express route was established in the late 1860s between Walla Walla, Washington, and Missoula, Montana. From Rathdrum the rider headed northeast to Steamboat Landing, on Lake Pend Oreille where the mail was put on a steamer for transport to a relay station near Sandpoint. The first Northern Pacific depot appears on the right and the water tank is at the far left.
Rat-2-3

The McGinty Bar in Rathdrum, early 1900s. This bar is one
of many that operated in Rathdrum. The Brophy, Lee and
Jackson and Gordon Saloons were among those destroyed in
the 1884 fire. In 1890 the G. Jacobs and two of Bradley and
Butler's saloons were lost. In 1924 the last major fire burned
the remaining evidence of the prosperous town of Rathdrum.
Rat-4-1

*"I remember the 1924 fire. I watched it burn. They hooked the fire
hose up and hollered 'turn the water on' but they didn't have no
water. Two blocks on the south side of First Street burnt up. It started in an old wooden hotel right next to the drug store. They never
did find out what started it, but it was a nice big fire."*
—Leslie Cady

Rathdrum about 1910. In the distance, the fertile farm lands of the Rathdrum Prairie.
Rat-2-2

The first threshing machine on the Rathdrum Prairie, 1898.
James Casey of Hayden Lake operated his threshing machine
on the Rathdrum Prairie, traveling from farm to farm threshing grain. This type of equipment was too expensive for indi-
vidual farmers to own, so they would hire out the threshing.
Agr-1-17

Rathdrum 6th grade classroom, 1908. Superintendent Speorry
monitoring the classroom. This photo is part of a series of pho-
tos showing various school facilities in Rathdrum in 1908, the
same year the county seat was moved to Coeur d'Alene.
Rat-8-42

Hauling ponderosa pine near Rathdrum, early 1900s. In the 1880s a shingle mill was set up on lower Twin Lakes. Most shingles were made of cedar but about a third were made from yellow or ponderosa pine. Many of the early settlers on the Rathdrum Prairie had no water except what was collected from their roofs after a rainfall. Troughs at the eaves drained rainwater into cisterns and this was the domestic water supply for family and animals. Cedar shingles tended to discolor the water so settlers wanted roofing that would leave the water clear and free of the taste of wood. Ponderosa pine shingles met this requirement.

Log-3-38

Kootenai County Courthouse from 1889 to 1908. The tall
wooden building served as the courthouse in Rathdrum.
Rat-10-12

The record vault at Rathdrum.
When the battle began to remove
the county seat from Rathdrum
the community made a strong
case for keeping it by taking a
series of photographs showing
how modern and safe the facilities were. In 1885 there was an
attempt to remove the county seat
from Rathdrum and local citizens
guarded the record vaults in fear
that Coeur d'Alene citizens would
take the records.
Rat-10-10

Idaho and Washington Northern Depot at Rathdrum, about 1910.
The Northern Pacific was the first railroad through Rathdrum in
1882. The Idaho and Washington Northern arrived in 1908.
TRR-15-9

Street scene in Rathdrum, 1908. Just prior to moving the county seat
to Coeur d'Alene.
Rat-1-2

Rathdrum Public School. This three-story high school was built in 1908 and included four large classrooms, library, laboratory and gymnasium.
Rat-8-1

Rathdrum State Bank, about 1908. Speculation about the future prosperity of the area, as well as a growing agricultural economy, encouraged many to open businesses in Rathdrum.
Rat-3-22

Bradbury's store about 1885. Rathdrum was a supply point for
miners, on their way to the Coeur d'Alene mines, but when
the Spokane Falls and Idaho Railroad built its line from Hauser
Junction to Coeur d'Alene in 1886, Rathdrum lost much of its business. Prior to 1886, miners would leave the Northern Pacific train at
Rathdrum, take a stage to Coeur d'Alene where they would board a
steamboat up the Coeur d'Alene River to the Old Mission and then
continue by railroad to the mines.
Rat-5-2

The Bradbury Store. This was one of the first stores in Rathdrum. Pictured are E.H. Bradbury, Ernie Reinhart, Fred Bradbury, Dick Wright, Tom Ross, Helen Radner and Reverend Calbright.
Rat-5-3

BLACKWELL'S VISION: SPIRIT LAKE

Prior to the platting of the town of Spirit Lake in 1907, the area was heavily timbered and sparsely settled. The development of the Panhandle Lumber Company by Frederick Blackwell and Associates was the beginning of Spirit Lake. In 1907 the Spirit Lake Land Company was formed to sell lots. Within two years the town had grade schools, a high school, organized sports, churches, and fraternal organizations. They also had electric lights, cement walks, and telephones. Spirit Lake was promoted as an ideal place to live and visit.

Railroad construction above Spirit Lake, 1907. The Idaho and Washington Northern Railroad was constructed to bring equipment to the Panhandle Lumber Company and then to carry the lumber to market. Construction began at two points, Spirit Lake and Spokane.
TRR-15-11

Previous page: ***Spirit Lake from Mt. Spokane.*** Spirit Lake was named from a Native American legend, which explains the Salish name "Tesemini", meaning "Lake of the Spirits". It is said that an Indian chief's daughter eloped with a young brave. The father pursued them and out of fear of being separated the brave took the girl into his arms and jumped into the lake. Their bodies were never found. They believed that "Tesemini" carried them away.
Spi-1-4

Panhandle Mill. F. A. Blackwell owned controlling stock in this mill, which cost over $300,000 to complete in 1907. The Idaho and Washington Northern Railroad provided transportation for the lumber to outside markets.
Mil-16-20

Railroad men in front of the Panhandle Lumber Co. The workers who constructed the mill and the railroad lived across the lake at the mouth of Brickel Creek.
Mil-16-18

Hauling logs by sled to Spirit Lake, about 1908. During the winter sleds were used to transport logs to the Panhandle Lumber Company.
Log-3-35

Log flume near Spirit Lake, about 1915. An elaborate ten-mile-long flume system was built on Brickel Creek to transport logs to Spirit Lake, where they were towed to holding ponds to be sorted and sent on to the Panhandle Lumber Company. Most of the timber for the Panhandle Lumber Company came from the east slope of Mt. Spokane.

Log-1-51

Logging camp at Brickel Creek near Spirit Lake, about 1910.
The Industrial Workers of the World formed in 1905 to organize workers into "One Big Union" by industry instead of by
specific craft or trade. In the spring of 1917, lumberjacks and
mill workers in North Idaho joined a strike of 50,000 Pacific
Northwest woodworkers led by the IWW. They demanded the
eight-hour day, no work on Sundays, clean bunks and cook
shacks, toilets and laundry rooms, good treatment of the horses, lights in the bunkhouses with tables for reading, medical
care and no blacklisting of union men.

The strike paralyzed the timber industry in North Idaho for
several months as whole camps slowed down or stopped
work altogether. By fall of 1917 the timber companies, unwilling to grant demands, and unable to continue work, petitioned Governor Alexander to call out the National Guard.
Aided by local law enforcement agencies and timber industry
police, federal troops marched into the IWW halls in Spirit
Lake, Sandpoint, Bonners Ferry, St. Maries and Spokane. They
destroyed the halls and rounded up Wobblies (IWW members)
and put them in "bullpens" (make-shift jails). The strike continued until spring, 1918, when the 8-hour day was instituted.
Log-6-65

Panhandle Lumber Company after the 1939 fire. On Aug. 5, 1939, a fire began on Mt. Spokane and by August 11 the fire reached Spirit Lake. The lumberyard, dry shed, railroad round house and forty million feet of lumber were burned. This marked the end of the Panhandle Lumber Company and the decline of the Spirit Lake economy.
Mil-16-30

F.A. Blackwell house in Spirit Lake, 1916. F.A. Blackwell formed the Panhandle Lumber Company and brought the railroad to Spirit Lake. He was said to be as honest as the day is long and his dream was to see a perfect town developed in Spirit Lake.
Spi-7-3

Spirit Lake Fourth Street, about 1907. Spirit Lake was built on land speculation and the promise of a prosperous lumbering industry.
Spi-2-15

"During the years 1908 and 1909 the village of Spirit Lake saw its most rapid growth. Buildings went up overnight. This is not an overstatement as after the men came home from work, they would help each other put up small tarpaper shacks, working far into the night. When you would look around in the morning, many times, you could see a shack where there had been an empty lot the night before. The hammering and sawing started around four-thirty in the morning so it was impossible to try to sleep after that time."
—Chester Phillips

South side of Maine Street looking west, 1907. The Spirit Lake Land Co., on the left, was newly formed at the time of this photograph. It was organized to provide for the sale of land and establish a light, water and sewer system. They also promised to grade the streets, put in cement sidewalks and plant trees between the sidewalk and street.
Spi-2-11

Spirit Lake Cafe, the first building in Spirit Lake, about 1907. Mr. Bacon standing in the doorway.
Spi-4-2

Spirit Lake Meat Company, located on the north side of Maine St. between Fourth and Fifth, 1908. M.J. Williams had the first meat market in Spirit Lake.
Spi-5-7

Below: *Maine Street winter 1913.* The Toggery Clothing Store is to the right of the Mill Bank building. H. Krech Real Estate is on the left. Mr. Krech was involved in many ventures in Spirit Lake, including the first mercantile store and the first brick building. Many of the earlier wooden buildings were replaced by brick in response to the growing economy.
Spi-2-7

Another view of Maine Street the winter of 1913. The city was snowed in during this winter and even train service was stopped.
Spi-2-6

Hotel Grand and Bar on the corner of Fourth and New Hampshire, 1910s. A variety of service and merchandising businesses were built to serve the new community.
Spi-4-1

United Presbyterian Church, about 1910. By 1916 Spirit Lake had four churches.
Spi-9-3

NO-30-MASONIC TEMPLE, SPIRIT LAKE, IOA.

The Masonic Temple, built by D.J. Wright about 1910. Spirit Lake prided itself on having many of the social amenities of modern life including several fraternal organizations and an opera house.
Spi-7-2

Spirit Lake Public School, 1908. Construction began in April 1908.
Spi-8-9

Preparing to move during the 1939 fire. As the fire crept close
to the town, people began moving their belongings into the
street to await transportation away from the fire.
Spi-17-1

The Spirit Lake baseball team. On the right is Jack Ellersick.
Spirit Lake had an organized baseball team for many years.
Rec-4-33

Spirit Lake Boat House, 1910. This area, known as
the Chautauqua Grounds, was open to the public as a
recreational area. There was a bathhouse, tennis court,
amusement booths and a dance pavilion.
Spi-15-6

Mrs. Paul Clagstone ready for fishing at Spirit Lake. Fishing was a popular pastime at Spirit Lake. The bugs were often very bad and here Mrs. Clagstone is wearing netting to protect her face.
Rec-3-58

Below: ***The tour boat "Echo" on Spirit Lake, about 1910.*** The Spirit Lake Navigation Company offered steamer tours and rented rowboats and canoes. Boats were needed to get to the various campsites. One such camp near the head of the lake, Shingobe Park, rented house tents.
Spi-16-4

The Railroad Park. The Idaho and Washington Northern Railroad not only provided transportation for lumber out of the area but also brought tourists and newcomers to town. The park lined both sides of Maine Street leading into town. Trees, shrubs and flowers were planted to make this park a main attraction for train travelers coming to Spirit Lake. *TRR-15-3*

Chautauqua Bridge. This 918-foot timber piling bridge was built in 1912 and used for forty years. A Chautauqua was a traveling group that featured educational shows in the form of ballets, concerts and lectures. From 1912 to the Depression era this was an annual event in Spirit Lake. *Spi-15-4*

HEAVENLY WATERS: TWIN LAKES

The first residents at Twin Lakes were loggers and home-steaders. By 1910 Twin Lakes had become a popular camping and recreational spot. People began building summer cabins and commuting from Spokane, Rathdrum and other communities for weekends and vacations. The railroad provided passenger and freight service to Twin Lakes and hotels and resorts were built around the lake to accommodate the tourists.

Lower Twin Lakes looking southwest from the top of Echo Cliff. Excelsior Beach can be seen along the base of the hill to the right and Echo Beach is directly across the lake where a few buildings stand. Hart's Island is in the distance.
TL-1-1

Opposite page: ***The narrows on Twin Lakes, a popular boating spot, 1918.*** A legend tells that a large sturgeon swooping from one lake to the other formed the channel between the upper and lower lakes. In the background log booms are visible. Logs brought to the lake were fastened into log rafts and towed to the mills.
TL-5-12

Camping at Twin Lakes, August 1904. Prior to building cabins
at Twin Lakes people camped. Many used large canvas tents
set up with locally cut poles.
TL-4-4

The Lewis Family and friends on the porch of their cabin at Excelsior Beach in 1908. The Lewis and McInturff families were the first to build a cabin at Excelsior beach. In 1908 those camping and building cabins named the beach Excelsior, meaning "higher up" because it was so heavenly.
TL-3-7

Swimming at Twin Lakes, 1900.
TL-5-9

***Idaho and Washington Northern Depot at Twin Lakes, about
1910.*** The IW & N was known as the Pend Oreille River
Route, the first train arrived in Twin Lakes January 25, 1908.
The railroad combined freight service to the timber country with passenger service to the lake. In the summer there
were commuter rates of $1.50 for the one hour round trip to
Spokane. Six trains a day ran until the automobile became
popular. Daily trips continued until about 1920.
TRR-15-8

The train stop known as Sturgeon. In 1916 Sturgeon was the
name of a train stop near Twin Lakes. At one time Twin Lakes
was known as Sturgeon.
TRR-15-15

The Gonzaga Camp at Twin Lakes. The Gonzaga Camp was
acquired by Gonzaga University in 1912 for use as a recreational retreat. Jesuits taking breaks from books and studies
would stay for two days to a week at a time relaxing, swimming, and boating on the lake. The camp had a small chapel
and cabins in which the Jesuits stayed and cooked their meals.
Local residents can recall hearing them singing while they
boated on the lake in the evening.
TL-2-17

The Twin Lakes Park Hotel, 1915.
TL-2-16

Summer cabins at Twin Lakes in the early 1900s. There were
many cabins and rooms for rent around Twin Lakes to serve
the tourist trade. Among them were Dellars Resort, Echo
Beach Resort, Lilac Lodge, White Hotel, Tom Bates Resort,
and the Ravigney Hotel, later known as the Hook Hotel.
TL-3-10

The road along Twin Lakes near Echo Beach, 1918. The county
built a highway next to the railroad right of way in 1907.
Trd-1-43

Miley's Resort, about 1940. In 1921 Mr. and Mrs. Miley
bought the Echo Beach Resort from Henry G. Reiniger. They
operated this resort for many years.
TL-2-1

Merle Miley (left), Howard Hensley (husband of photogra-
pher Marianne Hensley) and unidentified friend cutting ice on
Twin Lakes, 1960s. The Mileys owned an icehouse and supplied the residents of Twin Lakes. Ice was cut from the lake
and stored in an icehouse, which was packed with sawdust
to keep it frozen. Electricity came to Twin Lakes in 1938, but
they continued to cut ice for many years.
TL-6-1

DREAMS AS DEEP AS LAKE PEND OREILLE: BAYVIEW AND LAKEVIEW

H-140 Bayview, Idaho, on Scenic Bay

Prior to Euro-American settlement on Lake Pend Oreille, Native Americans who, lived by hunting, fishing and gathering berries, occupied the shores and surrounding lands.

During the late 1880s Steamboat Landing served as a major transfer point for travelers and goods going to various points along Lake Pend Oreille and as a connection point via overland stage eight miles to the Northern Pacific Railroad station at Athol. Squaw Bay was a small resort settlement, fishing village and winter headquarters for hunters and trappers.

In 1903 four lime quarries and five limekilns were in operation along the north side of Squaw Bay. Because Squaw Bay did not freeze over completely it proved to be an ideal location for boating traffic and became a major transfer point for tourists, supplies and products. In 1911 the Spokane-International built a spur line, called the Coeur d'Alene and Pend Oreille Railroad, to the docks in Squaw Bay.

At the same time the Prairie Development Company of Spokane took on the project of laying out the new town site of Bayview with graded streets, sidewalks, curbs and a city water supply.

Due to its close proximity to Spokane and the railroad Bayview soon became a favorite tourist spot, shipping and distribution point for the mines and quarries located at the south end of Lake Pend Oreille.

It was only two years after the limekilns and quarries ceased operation that the U.S. Government opened Farragut Naval Training Station in 1942. The south end of Lake Pend Oreille once again proved to be a prime location for boating activity.

Primarily hunters, trappers, and farmers utilized Gold Creek drainage until the 1883 discovery of gold brought hordes of prospectors into the area. Additional mineral findings along Granite Creek in 1886 brought nearly two thousand miners to the southeast end of Lake Pend Oreille. Then in 1888 William Bell located the Weber Mine, the first viable lead, zinc, and silver ore deposits.

Lakeview was one of the largest settlements, which sprang up overnight in order to keep up with the rush of miners and activity in the area. It had a post office, school district and a variety of businesses. Before 1900, when Lakeview was at

Opposite page:
Bayview with Bernard Peak in the background, about 1920.
Scenic Bay was first known as Squaw Bay as early as 1894. The village in the bay was known as Squaw Bay. It was not until after the turn of the century that Bayview received its present name. Settled in the late 1860s, Pend Oreille City, is one of Kootenai County's oldest towns. It was located in Steamboat Landing (today 's Idlewild Bay).
Bay-1-18

its peak, the population was over 1,000 and it sported over fifteen saloons on the main street. Supplies, passengers and mail made their way to Lakeview by way of steamboats that connected with the Northern Pacific Railroad at Hope and at the transfer point at Steamboat Landing (Idlewild Bay) for the eight-mile stage line trip to the Northern Pacific Railroad depot at Athol.

Bayview School on the Russell property, about 1906. This school was used until 1912, when sealed bids were taken to build a new two-room frame school. It was fifty feet by fifty feet, with a sixteen-by-twenty-foot annex including an outbuilding.
Bay-5-1

The Wigwam Lodge. Originally called the Bayview Inn, the Wigwam Lodge, was built in 1910 by J. Grier Long. The Inn had twenty rooms, four baths, and rooftop gardens with flower boxes. When the name was changed to the Wigwam Lodge each room was given an Indian name and the history of the tribe placed on the inside of each door. The Washington Brick, Lime and Sewer Pipe Company had a company store in part of the hotel building from 1914 to 1919. During World War II the Lodge became part of the Farragut Naval Training Station. The building was razed in 1960.
Bay-2-1

Wiley's Boat Livery. After 1911, excursion trains arrived on
Sundays and holidays with up to 200 people. They came to
fish, swim and to explore the lake by boat. The first boat livery
in Bayview was owned by Wiley. The area along the waterfront between the ends of 5th and 6th streets is now known as
Boileau's Resort.
Bay-2-8

Bayview waterfront. In 1903 the Washington Brick, Lime and Sewer Pipe Company opened four lime quarries on the north side of Bayview under the management of August W. Johnson. In the photo where the smoke is rising is the location of the factory built to make barrels for the lime. Burlap sacks replaced the barrels and finally paper sacks were used for shipping. The *Northern* is at the railroad dock with a barge at the end of the dock. The rock crusher is above the railroad docks and Wiley's Boat Livery is in the right foreground. *Bay-2-11*

***Washington Brick and Lime Company along the north shore of
Squaw Bay (now called Scenic Bay) after 1911.*** Lime processing
began in the Bayview area in the late 1880's. In the early 1900s
the Washington Brick and Lime Company of Spokane built four
large draw kilns along the shore of Squaw Bay. These draw kilns,
which heated lime to 3,100 degrees, replaced the small conical kilns used in earlier lime processing operations. By 1905 the
plant was producing seventy-five barrels a day and shipping the
lime via barge or the steamboat *Bayview* to the Northern Pacific
railhead at Hope and the Great Northern railhead at Sandpoint.
In 1911 a spur of the Spokane International Railway was extended to Bayview. This encouraged the lime company to build a
fifth kiln. The quality of the lime deteriorated and by 1940 the
lime kilns and quarries were silent.
Bay-3-2

***View of the remains of the Washington Brick and Lime Company
and the Bayview waterfront.***
Bay-2-12

The Rustler at the railroad dock. In 1911 a spur of the
Spokane and International Railroad, called the Coeur d'Alene
and Pend Oreille Railroad, came to Bayview. This eliminated
the need to barge products to Hope to connect with the
Northern Pacific.
LPO-2-17

Delivery truck. Trucks like this connected the communities of Athol, Bayview and Rathdrum by transporting goods and passengers. *Trd-13-2*

The Farragut Village Office, 1943. Twenty-two thousand people helped build Farragut Naval Training Station in 1942. There were about fifty-five thousand men stationed at Farragut at any one time. Millions of board feet of lumber were needed as well as other goods and services. The navy built Farragut Village to house about two thousand civilian workers and their families. It had 115 buildings including apartments and dormitories, a five-hundred-seat auditorium for showing movies and holding church services, a school with grades one through eight, a dispensary, infirmary, beauty and barber shop, telephone exchange, post office and telegraph office and cafeteria. Buses ran to Coeur d'Alene every hour and two round trip trains went to Spokane every day. *FNT-3-25*

Lakeview, 1899. The photographer mistakenly labeled this photograph Lakeview, Washington, but Caro Lou Weber Bastion's house is in the right foreground and she lived in Lakeview, Idaho. Her dad's uncle, Fred Weber and S.P. Donnelly grubstaked Billy Bell, who discovered the Weber Mine in 1888. *LV-1-6*

Caro Lou Weber Bastion told Roy Ellis the following story:
"When Fred Weber left for Rathdrum to file his claim in 1888 he chartered the Western *and the* Northern *at Steamboat Landing in order to tie them up so others couldn't get over to Lakeview. When he returned from Rathdrum, after filing his claim, the whole beach at Lakeview was full of rowboats."*

Camping on Lake Pend Oreille. Even before the cement plant and lime kilns were in operation the lake was well known around the Northwest for its hunting, fishing, boating and camping opportunities.
LPO-3-4

HOTEL SWASTIKA UNDER THE MANAGEMENT OF THE SWASTIKA MINING AND DEVELOPMENT CO.

LAKEVIEW IDAHO

The Swastika Hotel at Lakeview. Built prior to 1900, this hotel was located on the north side of North Gold Creek away from the main part of town. Two ballrooms were available in the hotel, one for fancy balls and another for the lumberjacks. The Swastika Mining and Development Company owned a mine up Chloride Gulch, a tributary of Gold Creek, as well as the hotel. Many people would come to Lakeview from Bayview and Sandpoint by way of the steamboats *Northern* and *Western*. The hotel burned about 1915.

LV-1-15

Sheep offloading from the Rustler at Lakeview in 1921. Sheep grazed on stump ranges in the Lakeview and Cedar Creek area. In 1938 and 1948 large herds were again brought in to graze in the same area and on adjacent Forest Service lands. *LV-1-5*

The Spokane Portland Cement Company, about 1920. The
Spokane Portland Cement Company opened for operation in
1911 with the arrival of the Spokane and International Railroad
connection to Bayview. The cement was transported by barge
to the railroad at Bayview. Gales Bell, the son of William
(Billy) Bell, was the President of the Spokane Portland Cement
Company for many years. This view is looking south at the
cement plant from the vicinity of Lakeview.
LV-2-2

The Spokane Portland Cement Company.
LV-2-1

***The* Dora Powell** *pushing a barge.* The *Dora Powell* towed barges carrying railroad cars to the cement plant where they were positioned under chutes and filled with cement and then brought back to Bayview to connect with the Coeur d'Alene and Pend Oreille Railroad. This went on until 1928.
LV-2-6

The Lakeview Hotel and a pack train, about 1920. Because of
the rugged terrain and the lack of roads into the mountains near
Lakeview, supplies on their way to the camps on the other side
of Weber Summit in the Tepee Creek and Independence Creek
drainages, had to be unloaded at Lakeview and packed in by
horse and wagon.
LV-1-16

Ridge runners at the Smith Ranch near Lakeview, about 1930.
Left to right: Mrs. Smith, Jean Bell, Irene Smith and Alice and
Vivian Beauchine.
LV-2-5

*"The 'Smith Girls' didn't much care what people thought of them.
They were rough and ready. They farmed, they logged, operated a
sawmill...anything a man could do they could do better.*

*...I remember one day I had to take the mail boat across the lake to
Lakeview and I had to meet Jean Smith Bell with a delivery. I met
her at the dock and we had two 150-pound sacks of wheat to get up
the hill. I was struggling up the hill with one sack and she was right
behind me having less problems than I was."*
—Roy Ellis

THE LAND OF
AGRICULTURAL PARADISE:
ATHOL AND CHILCO

Located in the northern region of the Rathdrum Prairie, Colton seemed a likely location for a Northern Pacific Railroad station in 1882, and a center for a vast agricultural paradise. Renamed Athol, the area grew as lands were logged off and farms and orchards were developed. The community had a variety of businesses and services to accommodate the local growth. The depression reduced Athol's importance and the community declined until the 1940s when Farragut opened and created a temporary boost to the community.

Clarence S. Argo worked for the Milwaukee Railroad as an attorney in 1909, when he first came to North Idaho. He bought land around Chilco and made plans to develop an agricultural paradise. He encouraged others to come to the area, buy land and help develop orchards and vegetable truck farms. Many people did come to the area, and a farmers' union (a forerunner of the Grange) was formed. Many also lost their investments because of the killing frost that damaged the orchards. Photographs were taken to promote the project.

Opposite page: *View of Athol about 1910, Bernard Peak in the background.* The jack pine timber first attracted early settlers to Athol. Logging, milling and agriculture created prosperity. By 1903 there were many businesses including the Pacific Hotel, drugstore, blacksmith, jewelry store, restaurants, mercantile company, and a saloon. The school is the large brick building situated in the center of town. From the Northern Pacific depot at Athol one could take a stage eight miles to Bayview.
Ath-1-4

Birdseye-view of Athol, Idaho, from Water Tower.

View of Athol from the water tower. First known as Colton, the town was renamed Athol by a settler who came from Athol, Massachusetts. That town was named after a town in Scotland named for the Duke of Atholl.
Ath-1-1

The Methodist Episcopal Church at Athol. Erected in 1900, this church also served as the school until 1902.
Ath-1-2

The Athol School. The school was built about 1907 across the
street from the Methodist Church. This brick building was
used for all 12 grades until 1948 and then it was used for first
to eighth until 1968. The school was torn down in 1972.
Ath-3-1

The Athol Lumber Company. Incorporated Jan. 1, 1903, the Athol
Lumber Company was outfitted with a circular headrig, dry
kilns and planer. In 1906 the circular saw was replaced with a
band mill. 1912 marked the end of the Athol Lumber Company
when the planer burned.
Mil-7-11

Tractors hauling beets, c. 1905. D.C. Corbin (a major developer) established the Corbin Ranch located between Athol and Hayden Lake. With the help of Japanese laborers, who lived in camps between Hayden Lake and Athol, Corbin maintained orchards and grain, beet and hay fields. Seven hundred acres of beets were grown on land between Athol and Hayden Lake and they were trucked to his beet-processing factory at Waverly, Washington, to be made into sugar. The Rathdrum Prairie fields grew high yields of beets but the gravelly soil produced beets with stones in them, which damaged the factory knives at Waverly, which caused the operation to close in 1910.
Agr-1-13

"When I was a kid I remember seeing 30 or more slip wagons out behind the shop on the Rickel Ranch. Field workers would cut the tops off the beets and then put them into these slip wagons. The wagons had no wheels, but runners on them like sleds, and slats on the bottom to let the dirt filter out. The edges of the wagons weren't over 2 feet off the ground. Horses were used to pull the sled to the Spokane International Railway, which ran through the old Corbin Ranch."
——Robert Rickel

Chilco Falls, with the cement water holding pond below, about 1910.
Chi-2-4

"There used to be a store, a school and a farmers' union at Chilco. A promoter encouraged people to buy his irrigated orchard tracts of land. People sold their homes in the east to come out here. They lost everything. It was too frosty and it didn't prove out. Then they left. The school stayed open until consolidation and the railroad continued to stop to fill up at the water tank."
——*Kathryn McDaniel*

Chilco Falls before the construction began, about 1910. C. S.
Argo is standing on top of the Rimrock next to the falls.
Chi-2-2

Part of the Chilco Dam Project, about 1910.
Chi-2-9

The dam on top of the Rimrock at Chilco, about 1910. The lake
formed by the dam provided good fishing. C. S. Argo standing
on the dam.
Chi-2-8

Chilco Falls and cribbing, about 1910.
Chi-2-3

Looking west to Rathdrum Mountain. Notice the Spokane International Railway in the distance. The land has been cleared and is ready for planting, about 1910. Orchards were planted and it seemed Clarence Argo's dream of an agricultural paradise would be a reality, but frost killed the orchards and the project failed.
Chi-1-3

Chilco School. The Chilco School was built by C. S. Argo and began operation May 24, 1912. It was located on the prairie below the Rimrock and consisted of four classrooms.
Chi-1-5

GREEN CITY IN THE PINES: HAYDEN LAKE

Father DeSmet was among the first white men to visit and write about Hayden Lake and the Indians. The area was first homesteaded in the late 1870s by Mr. Strayhorn and three soldiers from Fort Sherman; Matthew Hayden, (who settled at present-day Honeysuckle Beach); John Hager (who settled at present site of the Hayden Lake Country Club), and John Hickey (present site of the Avondale Country Club). It is believed that Matthew Hayden and several homesteaders, who lived on the shores of the lake, played a game of 'seven-up' to determine who should name the lake. Hayden won the card game.

Beginning in the 1880s there were several small mining operations along the North Fork of Hayden Creek. By the early 1900s Hayden Lake was a thriving boomtown, with its economy based on agriculture, lumbering and recreation. The Coeur d'Alene & Spokane electric line railroad came in 1907, providing transportation to and from the area.

The Hayden Improvement Company purchased 145 acres and built the Bozanta Tavern and laid out a town site. The post office was established in 1907 and the first store, known as Monaghan's, was owned by Mr. Justis, of Honeysuckle Beach. Later other businesses developed near the south end of the lake as well as a sawmill owned by Mr. Wood and Mr. McGee.

The town of Hayden Lake shifted from its location near the lake and railroad to Government Way as automobiles replaced rails. The post office moved from the Bozanta Tavern to Hayden Village in 1959.

Previous page: ***Threshing machine on the Rimrock near Hayden Lake, 1898.*** The four Rose brothers owned this steam-powered stationary threshing machine. The engineer on the machine wearing a derby hat is Ernie Weeks. The Roses also had the first hay baler in the area. Early agricultural efforts in the Hayden Lake area consisted of growing hay and alfalfa and raising vegetables and fruits for the local markets and later for the canneries and packing plants.
Agr-2-13

Packing House at Dalton Gardens, 1920s. Apples, plums, cherries, strawberries and other berries were planted in the Hayden Lake area with good results. A growers' union was formed and a small packing plant was built after 1900. In 1923 a larger plant was built. Vegetables and poultry were also raised in the area with great success. Several years of killing frost in the 1930s destroyed many of the orchards.
Agr-6-1

First school in Hayden Lake, 1891. Miss Mary Crockett was the first full-time teacher and was paid twenty-five dollars a month to teach about twenty students. Many of the students rode horses or walked long distances to school, but few were ever tardy. *Edu-1-9*

Hayden Lake Church. This is believed to be to have been built in 1908. *Hay-5-1*

Logging ponderosa pine. Logging was done in the Hayden Lake area to supply the sawmill at Honeysuckle Beach. Frank and Charles Wood and Mr. McGee later sold the mill to M.D. Wright, who operated the mill until 1909. Several other mills operated around the lake in the late 1890s and early 1900s *Log-2-3*

Steamers on Hayden Lake, about 1910. At one time there were four steamboats on Hayden Lake. Frank Lee owned the first one, in 1904. The Hudlow Brothers, Alf and Robert, had the second steamer, and two boats were owned by Mr. Skinner. *TrW-22-4*

Hayden Lake boating and camping, about 1910. House tents and cabins were rented for $2.50 and upwards about 1910.
Hay-3-1

Before the Trolleys came, about 1905. Prior to the Coeur d'Alene & Spokane electric line railroad coming to Hayden Lake the only transportation was by horse or foot. In 1902 the cabins were known as the Avondale Cottages. This lakeside location has long been a favorite resort spot.
Hay-2-25

THE "RED HOUSE"
CHARLES M. AND LETTIE OIEN

Club House, Bozanta Tavern, about 1910. This was the Hagar homestead prior to the building of the resort. Bozanta Tavern manager Mr. Oien and his family on the porch.
Hay-2-39

"Some of the most interesting things I did as a young fellow, just ten or twelve years old, we used to ride the train out to Hayden Lake and get off at the station and hike down where Bozanta Tavern is. There was a roadway and there was docks down below. We'd catch the steamer there and go up to a place we owned on the lake. There were very, very few summer homes on the lake."
——Melvin Booth

The Depot at the Bozanta Tavern, about 1910. In 1907 the electric railroad was extended from Coeur d'Alene to Hayden Lake. This provided easy transportation for agricultural produce and timber out of the area. It also brought trainloads of tourists to the resort.
TRR-1-61

Bozanta Tavern, 1910. Architect K.K. Cutter designed the resort and J.C. Olmstead, designer of New York City's Central Park and many of Seattle's parks, was the landscape architect for the 158-acre project. The resort was built in 1907 with thirty-five guest rooms and twenty summer cottages, kitchen, dining rooms, clubhouse, playground, and dancing pavilion. Guests could occupy themselves with fishing, golf, tennis, ring quoits, croquet, box ball, brist, and baseball.
Hay-2-15

Golfing at Bozanta Tavern, 1912. This area was originally Mr. Hager's orchard. The trees were removed to make way for a horseracing track. In 1907 a nine-hole golf course and a racetrack were available to the tourists. By 1912 the racetrack was removed and the golf course was enlarged to eighteen holes, making this the first eighteen-hole golf course in the state of Idaho.
Hay-2-22

Clark House. F. Lewis Clark, a Spokane millionaire, built the house on the south end of Hayden Lake in 1909. It was the largest house in Idaho at the time it was built. The walls were decorated with hand-painted wallpaper and the landscaping cost $2,000. Mr. Clark disappeared five years after the house was built. The home was used as a restaurant, a hotel, a boys' home, a convalescent home during WWII and a bed and breakfast. *Hay-12-5*

Drilling for Oil, Hayden Lake Rimrock, 1926-27. C. C. Worst leased his property on the rimrock to an oil drilling company in hopes of discovering oil. The company also drilled at Ramsey on the Rathdrum Prairie, but nothing was found at either location. *Min-2-22*

POST FALLS: A TOWN TO RIVAL SPOKANE FALLS

Long before Post Falls came to be a town settled by lumbermen and farmers, it was a Coeur d'Alene Indian village known as Q'emiln (throat of the river). The Indians had prosperous farms in the Post Falls area until 1878, when they moved to the reservation at DeSmet.

In 1871, a German immigrant from Illinois, Frederick Post, came through the Post Falls area. Realizing the importance of the upper falls on the Spokane River he began work on a sawmill, but before it was completed he went to Spokane to build the area's first gristmill on the lower falls in 1876.

In 1880 Mr. Post returned and completed his sawmill, which would be the first commercial sawmill in Kootenai County. During the early 1880s mining boom of the Coeur d'Alene region, D.C. Corbin built a spur of the Northern Pacific Railroad from Hauser Junction through Post Falls to Coeur d'Alene. Frederick Post sold his water rights to a group of mine owners, who eventually sold to the Washington Water Power Company. Post Falls began to grow and change very quickly in 1890 and by 1900 the little community was so dynamic that it was said to rival Spokane Falls.

Previous page: *Treaty Rock.* Located south of the intersection of Seltice Way and Compton Street in Post Falls, Treaty Rock is a large granite rock at the western edge of Treaty Rock Park. In 1977 Edgar and Gladys Seiter donated Treaty Rock Park to the City of Post Falls. Carved on the rock are the words, "June 1,1871, Frederick Post" and Indian pictographs or rock paintings, done sometime after 1730. Local legend has fostered the belief that the pictographs and petroglyphs represent a treaty between Andrew Seltice and Frederick Post. After signing a treaty in 1889 at DeSmet with the U.S. Government, Chief Seltice signed a title of abstract stating that in 1871 he had sold land to Frederick Post. In 1894 Frederick Post received title from the Government to 298 acres including the town site, waterpower site and land on the south side of the river.
His-1-17

Overview of Post Falls looking north on Spokane Street. Before 1900 a variety of businesses operated in Post Falls including a boot and shoe store, dry goods and clothing emporium, hardware and jewelry stores, meat market, a hotel, two livery stables, two blacksmith shops, a bakery, and a newspaper. The Kamps' home is in the right foreground.
PF-14-3

Frederick Post's waterpowered sawmill, 1880-1902. The Post sawmill was finished
in 1880. Post leased the mill to the Bish Lumber Company off and on until Mr.
Bish drowned in the falls in 1892 at which time it was leased to the Bader Lumber
Company. In 1894 Frederick Post sold the mill to the Spokane and Idaho Lumber and
Manufacturing Company, H.M Strathern, president. The mill Post built was destroyed
by fire in 1899, but the sawmill and planing mill were rebuilt. The Post Falls Sash and
Door Company operated on the site until it was destroyed by fire in 1902.
Mil-11-6

Cable Milling Company, before 1900. Before the upper falls
were harnessed to the production of electric power early pio-
neers used them to operate a sawmill and a flour mill. On the
left is a wooden grist mill called the Cable Roller Mills, built
by the Dart Brothers in 1899. It remained in operation until the
Washington Water Power Company purchased it in 1909. The
year before WWP purchased the mill site, the milling company
had completed many improvements including concrete work,
new gates, a millrace and canal. The mill site consisted of the
large mill buildings, grain elevators, waterpower plant, railroad
spurs and several acres of land adjacent to the falls at the time it
was sold.
Mil-11-12

Cable Roller Mills. This flour (grist) mill was owned and operated by the Dart Brothers and J.H. Sullivan from 1899 until
Dec. of 1902, when it was sold to the Cable Milling Company
owned by E.J. Dyer, E.G. Russell, B.O. Graham and L.H.
Graham. The building in the foreground is probably the 200-
horsepower water power plant that produced electricity for
the mill's lights. The large building on the right horizon may
be the Post Falls School built in 1890. Frederick Post's sawmill
was located at the upper (little) falls, immediately upstream
from the flour mill on the same side of the Spokane River. In
June of 1909, WWP purchased the Cable Milling Company and
the waterpower plant site thereby securing control over the
falls and adjoining land.
Mil-11-16

***Post Falls Coeur d'Alene & Spokane electric line train depot,
about 1912.*** The Coeur d'Alene and Spokane Railway, known as
the interurban and as the electric line, ran several times a day
from Spokane to Coeur d'Alene from 1903 to 1940.
TRR-1-58

Employees of the Post Falls Lumber and Manufacturing Company. Mr. Strathern owned the company and the employees were known as Strathern's men. The company operated from 1905 to 1919.
Mil-11-18

The Idaho Lumber and Manufacturing Company, about 1900.
The lathe and planing mills, and sash and door factory were housed in the rear.
Mil-11-17

Wooden irrigation flume, 1920. This wooden flume is a section of what was known as the "Corbin Ditch," built by D.C. Corbin in 1905. By 1918 the irrigation system carried water to 33,000 acres of farm land. D.K. Mathews used to ride his bike along the right side of the flume on top of two planks, looking for trouble spots. "Troubleshooter" for the ditch used the house on the island (right side of photo).
PF-1-11

Building the Corbin Ditch. Fresnos and horses were used on the north side of the Spokane River to smooth out the route of the irrigation ditch. The system had thirty-four miles of ditch and fifty-four miles of lateral canals extending from the Spokane River to the land north and west of the river. Many small communities emerged as a result of the newly irrigated lands. *Agr-12-14*

Picking beans. The Rathdrum Prairie and the Spokane Valley provided produce for the local canneries. *Agr-2-18*

Seiter's Cannery, 1940. In 1935 Gladys and Edgar Seiter opened a cannery in the old harvester factory at Post Falls. They remodeled and enlarged the buildings to include the processing of cherries, pumpkin, beans, tomatoes, apples, plums and their famous apple butter along with cider vinegar. Seiter's Cannery contracted out for acres of pumpkins, beans, tomatoes, and other vegetables in order to have an adequate supply for the cannery. This location served growers from Spokane, McGuire, Dalton Gardens, Hayden Lake and Post Falls for thirty-eight years. *PF-6-3*

Control panel of the Washington Water Power plant at Post Falls. Prior to 1900 a group of mine owners purchased the power site at Post Falls from Frederick Post in order to control access to power for the Silver Valley mines. The Washington Water Power company eventually purchased the power site and built lines from Spokane to Burke by 1903. By 1906 the Post Falls power station was complete.
PF-15-20

Above: *The Post Falls Washington Water Power Powerhouse.* The building on the right housed turbines for generating power. The building in the middle was for the control panel operators so they could look down the river. The building on the left held the transformers. The small building was the blacksmith shop, once operated by Nick Lindberg.
PF-15-13

District Number 7 School in Post Falls, 1890. The district was officially formed in 1886 and the school was built in 1890 at the northwest corner of Mullan Road and Spokane Street. At that time Post Falls had five hundred citizens. The building was last used as a residence before it burned in 1930.
PF-8-3

Post Falls School, the third public high school. Built in 1906 this concrete block building housed fifth through twelfth grades. The center building held 1st through 4th grades. The building on the far right was the gymnasium, added in 1913-14. Over half the construction was done by Mr. Rutledge's manual training class. The gym burned down in 1957.
PF-8-4

McGuire School. Built in 1911, this cobblestone school served
the community until 1948 when the Pleasant View, Cedar
Creek, McGuire and East Greenacres Schools were consolidat-
ed into the Post Falls School District. This building survived
into the late 1980s.
PF-8-15

Alan Racetrack Grandstand, May 1912. From 1910 to 1913 the Coeur d'Alene Fair and Racing Association operated the Alan Racetrack at Ross Point. The Coeur d'Alene & Spokane electric line railroad stopped outside the gate, bringing passengers from Spokane and Coeur d'Alene. With over five thousand people present at a single race, this was one of the most popular tracks in the Northwest. Horse racing was outlawed after 1913, at which time the track was used for boxing and other events until the grandstand burned in the late 1920s.
Rec-8-1

"The Finish": Emily Lee, the winner, 1912. At certain times
of the season two hundred horses would be brought in from
Montana bringing the number of entries up to six hundred.
Rec-8-10

Post Falls Band, 1910. The band often played at the park band-stand, which was located near the present day City Hall. Bill Carter is playing the cornet, Link Hawthorne is playing the trombone, and John Enders is playing the tuba.
PF-11-4

Pleasant View Bridge, the Plonske children. This is one of the bridges that connected the south side of the Spokane River to Post Falls. These bridges were important to the south side as their link to community services and social activities. *TRR-1-41.*

The first Green's Ferry Bridge, 1912. Mr. and Mrs. C.A. Whitaker and Mrs. Harvey Davy standing on the bridge, which was built in 1907. It was located about one and one-half miles upstream from Post Falls. John Green first operated a ferry at this location in 1890. In 1895 he sold his ferry and property to the Whitakers, who continued operating the ferry until the bridge was built.
TRR-1-31

Cyrus Hart with his U.S. mail cart, about 1900. In 1887 a post office was established at the town of Post, also known as Upper Falls. In 1890 the name was changed to Post Falls. Post offices were often located in mercantile stores.
PF-10-1

26-881 - STREET SCENE - POST FALLS - IDAHO - Sept. 9 - 1936 — photo by Leo's Studio —

Downtown Post Falls, Sept. 9, 1936. Spokane Street.
PF-2-1

Interior of Farmers Trading Company on Spokane St., 1930s.
Alf Webster, right, and John Webster, left. The Webster brothers
owned the store.
PF-5-1

The Farmers Trading Company, 1932.
PF-5-3

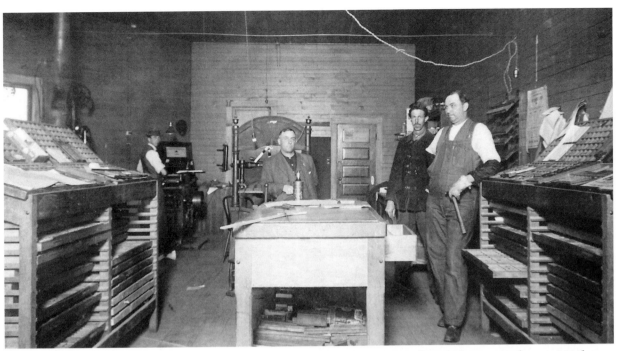

Post Falls Advance. Bill Carter, on the right, was the publisher of the Post Falls Advance. Typesetting trays and presses are visible. These were the days when all the letters were set by hand. *PF-3-2*

The Pony Saloon, about 1890. The building on the right is M. Born and Company, Merchant Tailors. *PF-4-1*

View of the Falls, early 1910s. The Falls have always been a
popular recreational spot. Here a couple are taking in the view
of the Washington Water Power dam built in 1906, the lumber
and manufacturing company built in 1905, smoke stack of the
boiler house, the city water tank on the right of the burner and
the mill water tank on the left above the mill. The Post Falls
bridge at Spokane Street is in the background.
PF-1-34

Overview of Post Falls, 1908, taken from Ford Rock.
PF-14-4

"*I knew Mr. Post very well. He was awfully nice. I can remember what he looked like. Had whiskers, you know men wore whiskers in those days. He was very much on keeping up the churches and things like that, you know, and he was awful good to his men. They had a little cave on the other side of the river that he fixed up for a picnic ground. The cave there was real cute. My father was helping do everything that Mr. Post wanted him to do.*"
——Josephine Hollins

COEUR D'ALENE: THE NEWPORT OF THE WEST

The confluence of Coeur d'Alene Lake and the Spokane River was a gathering place for the Coeur d'Alene Indians. They knew it as Yap-Keehn-um and they camped here with the Pend Oreille, Flathead and Kalispell Indians in the spring and fall to fish for salmon and to socialize. In 1842 Jesuits came to provide religious teachings to the Natives and eventually to establish a mission further to the east. Trappers, traders and surveyors such as General Isaac Stevens, looking for a northern route of the railroad, and John Mullan, the builder of the Mullan Road, passed through Coeur d'Alene. But it was not until the summer of 1877 when General William T. Sherman selected the site for a Fort that the area changed substantially. Established and garrisoned in the spring of 1878, Fort Coeur d'Alene included fifty-two buildings. This was the beginning of the city of Coeur d'Alene. Captain Sorenson was hired by the army to build the first steamer on Lake Coeur d'Alene and retained as the Captain. The *Amelia Wheaton* hauled hay from the Coeur d'Alene River area to the fort.

With the discovery of vast mineral resources in the Coeur d'Alene Mountains in 1883 an influx of traffic came through Coeur d'Alene. People came to Rathdrum on the Northern Pacific Railroad, took a stage to Coeur d'Alene where they boarded the *Amelia Wheaton* and traveled up the Coeur d'Alene River. In 1886 D. C. Corbin and associates built the Spokane Falls and Idaho Railroad, a branch from the Northern Pacific at Hauser Junction directly to Coeur d'Alene, bypassing Rathdrum. In the same year the Northern Pacific Railroad built the steamer *Kootenai* to transport the bulk of the freight that went to the mines.

The following year (1887) Coeur d'Alene was incorporated as a city. Tony Tubbs and other early settlers staked off their homesteads into town lots and sold them to the new arrivals. The *Coeur d'Alene Press*, a weekly paper, began in 1892.

Although the Fort was gone by 1901 the community continued to thrive. The major railroad lines came through Coeur d'Alene, a number of large steamboats were built as well as smaller craft, and a variety of industries developed, including lumbering and tourism. By 1920 five transcontinental railroads served Coeur d'Alene.

Opposite page: *Coeur d'Alene from Tubbs Hill, late 1890s.* The major brick buildings on Fourth and Sherman were built by this time. The Northern Pacific spur on Third Street was completed in 1886. Ore from the Coeur d'Alene Mining District was brought to Coeur d'Alene by steamer and transferred to the railroad. The round building on the left is a dance pavilion. The Coeur d'Alene Inn is behind the pavilion. *CDA-9-9*

Coeur d'Alene from Tubbs Hill, 1905-1908. In 1900 the population was 500 and by 1908 it was 8,000. With the newfound prosperity in the timber and mining industries many new brick buildings were built. The Hotel Idaho (later the Desert Hotel) was built in 1905 on First and Sherman to serve the growing tourist industry.
CDA-9-19

Fort Sherman from Blackwell Hill. Fort Coeur d'Alene was established in 1878 to keep peace between the settlers and Native Americans and to keep the Mullan Road open. In 1887 its name was changed to Fort Sherman to honor General William Tecumseh Sherman who selected the site. A town grew up around the fort; many of Coeur d'Alene's early settlers were soldiers at the fort and named such places as Fernan, Hayden, and Best.
FSh-3-5

Maggie Hickey Groves' quote from Feb. 28, 1958 Coeur d'Alene Press: *"Mrs. Groves was 6 years old when her family came here in January, 1878, when her father, John Hickey, was one of the first soldiers to be stationed at Fort Coeur d'Alene. She remembers the present town site of Coeur d'Alene was all wilderness, the only residents of the area being the soldiers and their families residing in tents, and some Indians living in tepees along the Spokane River."*

Sherman Avenue looking west from between Fourth and Fifth streets, early 1890s. The telegraph lines have been installed, but the power lines were not installed until 1893. The earliest part of town was between First and Third streets. This was the newer section of town and the streets were widened out from Third Street east.
CDA-8-5

Looking west above Sherman Avenue, 1928. On the bottom left is the Russell Blackwell House and to the west is the William Dollar house. Across the street is the Frederick Blackwell House (he built the one across the street for his son). Next door is the J.C. White house. The mill at the base of Tubbs Hill operated until about 1931.
CDA-9-52

Fifth and Sherman, 1918. Cliff Barnum on the tractor. The City
Hall, on the left, was built in 1908.
TrD-4-16

Corner of Second and Sherman St., Coeur d'Alene, Idaho.

Southeast corner of Second and Sherman, 1910. Colquhoun Hardware Store with the Majestic theatre on the left. CDA-2-27

"At one time we had three movies here. As a matter of fact I saw Charlie Chapman walking right up there between Third and Fourth streets on the north side of the street. He had one of his special movies showing at the old Liberty Theatre and he was here swinging his umbrella and kicking his toes out. I saw that."
——Fred Murphy

Looking east on Sherman Ave. from First, about 1895. Notice the power lines along Sherman. They were installed in 1893. The Coeur d'Alene Inn was previously called the Lakeside Inn. *CDA-8-2*

Looking north from Sherman Ave. up Second Street. Hotel Normoyle, Lafferty Bakery and the bank on Second and Sherman are visible. Second Street was an active business district. *CDA-8-28*

Coeur d'Alene waterfront between First and Second streets, about 1905. The Idaho Hotel is on the left. The Franklin Hotel located in the Flat Iron Building burned in 1908. The North Shore Motel, built in 1966 and later the Coeur d'Alene Resort were built on fill.
CDA-10-41

Interior of the Lafferty Bakery, about 1913. Benjamin S. Lafferty operated a bakery at 207 Sherman Ave. for several years. His son, A. B. Lafferty, operated the Lafferty Boat Works.
CDA-2-43

Coeur d'Alene Weaving Works, 819 N. Fourth, about 1912. The owner, Jarred H. Manly, is in the center.
CDA-17-20

Johnson's Boat Works, about 1890. P.W. Johnson came to Coeur d'Alene in 1889 and worked with Captain Sorenson building boats. They built about half of the boats on Lake Coeur d'Alene. In 1891 they became partners and Johnson eventually took over the business. The lakefront from Tubbs Hill to the City Park was an industrial area for many years.
TrW-20-4

Johnson's Boat Works, about 1890.
TrW-20-2

Lafferty Ship Fender Company. Located on Coeur d'Alene's downtown waterfront, this company made fenders for the Navy's ships during World War II. Left to right: Mrs. Sharples, Fred Williams and John O'Rielly
CDA-17-17

The block chopping crew at the Ohio Match Company, 1950.
During World War II as women entered sawmills to replace
men fighting in the War, the Lumber and Sawmill Workers-
AFL organized this new group of mill workers. State Industrial
guidelines that forbade women to lift more than sixty pounds
on a job, still prevented women from getting higher paying jobs.
These women made matches from small blocks of wood. The
mill, located at Huetter, sawed mostly white pine logs into thick
planks from which blocks for matchsticks were manufactured.
After 1945, when paper matches and cigarette lighters replaced
wooden matches, the sawmill shifted to general lumber produc-
tion. Management was taken over by Diamond International
Corporation in 1958. Bottom row from left: unknown, Evelyn
Pedey, Grace Moore, unknown, Gertrude Benson, unknown.
Second row from left: Grace Marcure, Nell Walker, Opal Wilson,
Minnie Edwards, Hulda Posness, Myrtle Allen, unknown, Mr.
Kinnier, Mr. O'Neil. Third row from left: Noleen Clark, Helen
Thompson, Georgia Jones, unknown, Cecile Johnson, unknown,
Daisy Wunderlich, unknown, unknown. Back row from left:
three men unknown, Marge Strange, unknown, Gladys Davis,
Thelma Oylie, unknown, Irene Catlin, Pearl Kinnier, Edith
Drissel, Sylvia Wruble and in the upper right is Estell Kinnier.
Mil-8-18

The Panhandle Brewery, about 1913. It opened as the Coeur d'Alene Brewery about 1909, but went broke and was reopened as the Panhandle Brewing Company in 1912 and operated until 1915. In 1917 the brewery went into bankruptcy. The building was used as a cannery for several years. Y-J Meats operated meat lockers there for many years. The building was torn down in 1965. It was located on River Avenue about half a block from the Spokane River.
CDA-17-1

The Coeur d'Alene Brewing Company, about 1910. The building was constructed between 1908 and 1910. The building contained close to six million bricks with walls seven bricks thick. On the site was a 300-foot well and an underground tunnel that carried mash to the Spokane River.
CDA-17-25

B.R. Lewis Lumber Company sorting platform, about 1905.
B.R. Lewis operated the mill from 1904 to 1907. In January
of 1909 Frank A. Blackwell bought the company. It was the
Blackwell Lumber Company until it closed May 4, 1937. Many
of the employees and assets were taken over by the Potlatch
Corporation.
Mil-1-2

Looking east from Blackwell Hill at the B. R. Lewis Lumber Company, c. 1900. Large stands of white pine brought the timber industry to North Idaho. By 1908 six large lumber companies were located in or near Coeur d'Alene. Fort Sherman buildings lay idle across the Spokane River.
Mil-1-14

Rutledge Timber Company. Mercury storage battery locomotives in the loading shed, about 1922. The Edward Rutledge Timber Company began operation in 1916 under the management of Huntington Taylor. George (Fritz) Jewett succeeded Taylor. Potlatch Corporation took over the mill in 1930 after years of unprofitable ventures, due mostly to the high transportation cost in the Marble Creek drainage area. Clarence Graue was manager from 1933 until 1958.
Mil-9-9

***The Relief Workers Protective Union demonstrating on Sherman
Avenue.*** Between 1930 and 1933 nearly 50 percent of woods
workers were laid off in North Idaho.
Lab-4-12

*"This is a crowd at the relief office trying to get some relief for people
who were hungry, didn't have fuel, didn't have warm clothing, didn't
have bedding and that sort of thing; being put out of their homes
because they couldn't pay rent.... We did go in there and demand to
see the files and see what was going on. They acted like we were nothing but a bunch of trash, because nobody had jobs or food or anything.
At this time the cops came down there to arrest the leaders, so every-
body that was there spoke up and said 'I'm a leader, I'm a leader' so
they didn't arrest anybody."*
—*Opal Brooten*

Caribou Mine about 1918. The mine was located on the south side of Beauty Creek and the Beauty Creek Road. Ten unpatented claims were first located in 1918 by W. J. Burns of the Caribou Mining Company. The main mineral body consisted of lead, zinc and pyrrhotite. The mine operated until about 1931. Cliff Barnum is sixth from the left.
Min-2-19

Field trip, Fourth and Sherman Avenue 1895. Coeur d'Alene's first school was at Fort Sherman. In 1884 Isaac Daly organized the first school district in the county.
Edu-3-1

Roosevelt School, 1905. Coeur d'Alene's first public school
was located on this site in 1884 in a log building. In 1905 it was
replaced with this brick structure.
Edu-1-10

***Central School at Seventh and
Wallace.***
Edu-1-30

Central School at Seventh and Wallace, about 1920. This was
Coeur d'Alene's first brick school building, built in 1901 at a
cost of $9,000. It housed grades one through twelve and had five
teachers and a principal with about 200 students. The teachers
made fifty dollars a month. The building burned in 1927.
Edu-3-16

*"I attended high school and played on the basketball team. Girls
played the same rules as the boys' team and often played at the same
school on the same day. One trip we went by electric line to Ross
Point and then by sleigh to Rathdrum. We enjoyed an oyster sup-
per and played our games, which ended by a fight between our
Superintendent H. H. Barton and a Rathdrum dentist."*
——*Hazel Cardwell*

*"I remember when the old Central School burned down, the sirens
were going, we ran down town to see the fire. That was quite a time.
We kids were tickled over that..."*
——*Mildred Olsen:*

Coeur d'Alene High School Football Team. They were the Idaho Panhandle Champions of 1925. The first football game was played on a gravel field on Blackwell Island in 1905. *Edu-4-19*

Classroom of the Academy of the Immaculate Heart of Mary, juniors and seniors, 1906-07. In 1905 the Fort Sherman hospital and the opera house were moved to Ninth and Indiana to serve as the sisters' home and a school for the children. *Edu-7-4*

Coeur d'Alene College, about 1916. The Lutherans founded the College in 1907 and it was commonly known as the Swedish College. They offered courses in six departments for men and women.
Edu-8-6

Marching Band on Sherman between Second and Third looking east, about 1935. Many of the buildings in the middle of the block on the south side burned.
CDA-13-10

***Coeur d'Alene baseball team in front of the Coeur d'Alene Inn,
1913.*** The earliest known baseball games in Coeur d'Alene were
played on the Fort Sherman grounds when soldiers still occupied the site.
Rec-4-12

Blackwell Park, about 1905. The park was built by F.A. Blackwell to accommodate the tourists arriving in Coeur d'Alene on the Coeur d'Alene and Spokane interurban railway. The park was located around the electric terminal near the lake front. *Rec-1-21*

Letter from Thomas Donica to Carrie Decker, March 12, 1903. "I guess if the electric line goes in, Coeur d'Alene will be a lively little berg this summer."

Racing Crew at the Coeur d'Alene Regatta, 1913. The first Regatta was held in 1913, and they continued as an annual event until the 1920s. Thousands of people came to Coeur d'Alene to take part in the festivities during the Fourth of July holiday. Activities included a Mardi Gras march through the streets, trick surfboard riding, motor boat races, music, dancing, fireworks, dashing and relay races, canoe tilting and races, log rolling, diving, and patriotic speeches.
From left: O. W. (Foxy) Edmonds, Bill Voelmeck, Frank Kann, and Lester Henderson.
Rec-17-2

Surfboarding at the Coeur d'Alene Regatta, c. 1920. John Featherstone and his partner Mirth MacArthur performing at the Regatta, Tubbs Hill in the background.
Rec-5-3

Grandstands at Tubbs Hill, about 1917. These stands were built to accommodate the crowds that came to watch the regatta activities over the Fourth of July holiday. They afforded a view of the entire course. Admission to the grandstand was fifty cents per adult. Coeur d'Alene's biggest regatta was in 1920 with 12,000 attending.
Rec-15-1

Coeur d'Alene City Beach, 1920s.
Rec-6-33

***Coeur d'Alene Eskimos'
Hockey Team at the
City Park.*** Established
in the 1930s, the
Eskimos' Hockey
Team mostly played
at the rink on Fernan
Lake. From left: Van
Richardson, Glen Nylen,
Gordon Reed, Ollie
Gillett, Don McDonald,
unknown, Trick Hall
from Kimberly, B. C.,
Harry Wilson, Earl
Faulkner. Kneeling are
Glen Gillett (left) and
Joe Whyte. First lady
on the left in the back is
Mrs. Joe Whyte.
Rec-39-2

HARRISON:
A TOWN OF
WATERFRONT
MILLS

The Harrison area was first occupied by Coeur d'Alene Indians. In 1890 settlers built a town site on a hillside on the west side of Lake Coeur d'Alene near the mouth of the Coeur d'Alene River. They believed the area was part of lands ceded by the Coeur d'Alene Tribe to the US government. When the 1891 survey revealed that the land was not among those ceded, it caused problems that took more than ten years to solve.

Addison Crane homesteaded the land and gave 99-year leases to people who wanted to build on his land. The town boomed and in July of 1891 thirteen new structures went up in a two-week period. The patents held by Addison Crane and his son William on their homesteads did not clear until February of 1909, finally giving them clear title to the lots they had already sold.

In 1890 the Oregon Railway and Navigation Company connected Harrison to Tekoa, Washington, in the west and to the Montana branch of the Northern Pacific Railroad in the east. The railroad transported Harrison's timbers, supplies, and passengers to the mining districts.

For a time, around the turn of the century, Harrison was the largest town in Kootenai County. The number of sawmills is disputed. Some sources say from eight to ten sawmills and up to seven shingle mills were in operation at one time. Many of these mills provided timbers for the mines in the Coeur d'Alene district.

The number of mills may be in dispute but it cannot be disputed that Harrison was a thriving community. Around 1900 the town boasted a 400-seat opera house. The 1911 City Directory reports a population of 1,250 and listed four churches, numerous fraternal organizations, two hotels, a weekly newspaper, and a high school and grade school employing seven teachers.

Previous page: ***Overview of Harrison, early 1900s.*** Millions of board feet of timber were stored in the lake at Harrison. The Coeur d'Alene and St. Joe rivers and Lake Coeur d'Alene were the major transportation routes for timber coming out of the area's forest reserves.
Har-2-5

In 1917 the Grant Lumber Company caught fire and the ensuing blaze consumed about half of Harrison's residential district, as well as many businesses. Much of the town was never rebuilt. Although the population never reached its former numbers Harrison continued to be a viable community. In the early 1950s the area around Harrison produced one hundred thousand bushels of wheat and thousands of beef cattle along with milk, eggs, chickens and butter. The lumber industry had long been the backbone of the community's economy. In 1953 Russell and Pugh and Connolly and Kroetch employed 110 people.

Community spirit continues today in the annual Harrison Picnic, which brings home many who have moved away. The first "Oldtimer's Picnic" was held July 26, 1953, and attracted 4,000 people.

Main Street Harrison, around 1910.
Har-4-20

Steamer Harrison at Harrison dock. The easiest way to get to Harrison was by water. The Oregon Washington Railway & Navigation Company, which absorbed the Oregon Railway and Navigation Company, constructed the 600-passenger steamer *Harrison* to provide transportation. People traveling from the west could take a train to Amwaco and board the steamer for a six-mile trip across the lake. This new route was about 25 miles shorter than the previous line that went further south through Tekoa and Plummer. In the early 1920s passenger service stopped, but they continued to haul freight until 1932, when the line was abandoned.
TrW-11-15

Railroad turntable on the south side of Harrison, 1932. In the early 1920s the Oregon Washington Railway & Navigation Company built a two-man turntable at Harrison near the Russell and Pugh Box Factory. Two to four trains a day transported passengers and freight from Harrison to Wallace. *TRR-9-7*

Ed Costello hauling logs on the Bell Canyon Road. Logs were hauled out by sleigh down Bell Canyon to Anderson Lake in the winter time. Logging operations on the Harrison Flats included flumes that transported logs to Lake Coeur d'Alene.
Log-3-52

St. Joe Lumber Company on the south side of Harrison, 1904.
Mil-6-19

Cameron Sawmill, 1901. The M. J. Sexton Mill moved from
DeSmet to Harrison in 1892. That same year the Cameron
brothers purchased it. With improvements and remodeling the
Cameron mill produced 75,000 board feet of lumber per ten-
hour shift. The facilities burned to the ground in 1902 and were
never rebuilt.
Mil-6-9

---

*"Five sawmills at Harrison have a combined capacity of about
250,000 feet of lumber a day, employing 280 men at the mills and in
the neighboring woods. Besides the sawmill there is a box factory and
two shingle mills. The logs for the mills are rafted down the St. Joe
and the Coeur d'Alene rivers, which tap a country that has an almost
inexhaustible supply of timber."*
——*Spokesman Review, January 21, 1902*

Duluth Mill fire, August 1916. In 1913 superintendent David
Lakin took charge of the newly constructed Duluth Lumber
Company. It was built on the site of the St. Joe Lumber
Company, which had burned in November 1908. The 1916
fire totally destroyed the Duluth Mill and it was never rebuilt.
Mil-6-22

Watching the Duluth Mill fire. When the mills caught fire
Harrison residents feared that the whole town could be
destroyed. People moved their belongings out of harm's way
and waited for the danger to pass.
Mil-6-21

Curly Cope and Ray Flatt carrying drinking water to mill workers, about 1917.
Har-6-1

"When I was growing up I was always out looking for jobs, something to earn some money . . . . At that time they had no drinking water piped down to the Export Lumber Company which was a big lumbering mill and we supplied the men with drinking water by carrying down these water bags full of spring water from up above on the hill." —Ray Flatt

Panoramic view of Harrison looking north.
Har-2-30

Harrison Main Street around 1910.
Har-4-17

Harrison Main Street. A. Jenson, Grocer, and Harrison's first
hotel on the right.
Har-4-16

The Hotel Harrison, about 1910. Grand balls were held and elegant dinners were served at the hotel.
Har-6-9

"Harrison has two good hotels, the Hotel Harrison being the leading one and is first class and up-to-date, with all modern conveniences"
——1911-1912 Polk Directory.

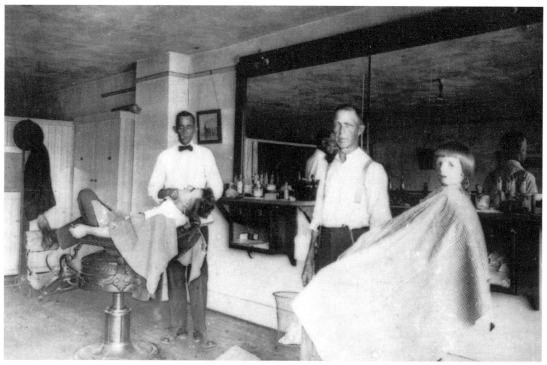

Milton Flatt's Barber Shop. Left: Charlie Cleveland and Milton Flatt.
Har-6-12

"This is the barber shop that I kept my Father supplied with tow-els, talcum powder, hair tonic and all that sort of thing and had the only bathtub--pubic bathtub--in the city at that time. One of my jobs was to keep the water hot by stoking the big stove that we had there hooked up to the water system, washing out the tubs after the individuals had taken baths in it, putting new towels in there and making it ready for the next customer. It was patronized quite heav-ily by the lumberjacks and the men who worked in the stores because there weren't many bathtubs inside homes at that time. It was quite a busy place. At that time my dad would keep the barbershop open until nine o'clock and the people who worked in the stores would not be able to come out and get their hair cut or get anything done until late at night." ——Ray Flatt

Lafferty's Grocery and Bakery Store, 1907. Brothers Benjamin and Charly Lafferty owned this store located near the Oregon Railway and Navigation railroad depot. The Lafferty Family lived in Harrison from 1899 to about 1910. Below, manager and co-owner Charly Lafferty inside the Lafferty store. *Har-5-7 (top) and Har-5-6 (bottom)*

Harrison's first hospital, around 1908. The hospital at Harrison
treated railroad and mill workers, loggers and accident victims,
as well as those affected during outbreaks of typhoid fever.
Typhoid outbreaks plagued Harrison every summer for many
years. When an outbreak occurred in August 1911, Dr. John
Finney was determined to find the cause. City water samples
sent to the state health laboratory in Boise came back positive
for typhoid bacilli. Harrison's water supply, installed in 1901 by
Powell's Water System, consisted of wooden pipes taking water
directly from the lake. A typhoid patient of Dr. Finney's, fearing
that he was close to death, confided that when the intake pipes
were laid near the docks, a section was broken during installa-
tion. Dr. Finney conducted a test by flushing mineral oil through
the system with a fire hose. An oily film on the water confirmed
that the pipe was broken. The break was close to the city's sewer
discharge and near docked steamers discharging toilet wastes.
The town took over operation of the water system and replaced
the wooden pipes with steel pipes set further out into the lake.
This put an end to the typhoid epidemics.
Har-6-6

Lakeview Hospital and Sanitorium, 1925. The Lakeview Hospital and Sanitorium, also known as the "Finney Hospital," was built by the Russell and Pugh Lumber Co. to care for sawmill workers. Between 1900 and 1917 Harrison had as many as three hospitals. This hospital continued to operate in Harrison until the 1930s.

Har-6-4

Essig's Drug Store and Post Office, 1901.
Har-5-9

Grant Lumber Company office in Harrison, 1917. The summer of 1917 was hot and dry. Early Saturday morning on July 24, 1917 mill workers reported a fire at the Grant Lumber Company. The Harrison fire department, along with able bodies from neighboring communities, was no match for the wind-driven fire. The fire burned for two days and destroyed about thirty residences, and sawmills.
Har-1-10

Street scene during the 1917 Harrison Fire.
Har-1-1

"The whistles of the mills along the waterfront awakened me early in the morning of another beautiful, hot, dry summer day. Both alarms were frightening to me and my brother Frayne. . . . A Pied Piper group of children following the Baptist minister and his wife came by and my mother insisted that my brother and I go with them. As we trudged barefooted down the soft dusty road we were joined by more children, some still in their night clothes. The whistles of the two lumber mills and one shingle mill added to the fear and dread in our little hearts. We hurried across the splintery bridge to the safety of a farm on the hill. . . . Back in town all the able-bodied men worked to save whatever they could, but it was a losing battle as first the board sidewalks, the steps that rose to the houses on the higher level and all but the big water tank at the top, just beyond the steps, smoldered and then were consumed in the advancing heat."-Sadie Harrison: Sadie was nine years old and living in Harrison during the 1917 fire.

***Telephone office in the Crane yard after the town burned in
1917.*** In 1902 Interstate Telephone built a line connecting
Harrison with points up the St. Joe and Coeur d'Alene rivers.
That same year the Rocky Mountain Bell Telephone Company
purchased the system and provided long distance service. After
the 1917 fire the telephone switchboard was temporarily located
in the Crane house. It was later moved to a second house on
Lake Front Drive, where it remained until the 1950s, when
General Telephone bought the system.
Har-1-7

Harrison School class, 1898-99. School District 29 was formed in 1895. Mr. Edelblute taught the first school class in Harrison in the Methodist Church building in the winter of 1895-96. The first school building was erected in 1896 and by 1903 there were 59 students in the district. Howard and Margaret Bald are in this class. *Har-8-1*

Harrison School, built in 1909, held all grades until 1956.
Har-8-6

***The Baptist Church Orchestra, Marsha Russell, Director, circa
1917.*** Front row, left to right: Lawrence Pugh, Herman Lemke,
unknown, Frances Pugh, Floyd Russell, Clyde York, Bernard
York, Harold Russell. Back row, left to right: John Diehl, Charles
Russell, Martha Russell, Lynn Russell, Joe Wark, Otto Mavis.
Har-9-1

RECREATION UNRIVALED

The Coeur d'Alene Region has long been recognized as a beautiful and wondrous place. In 1853 when General Isaac Stevens passed through the area he gave the following report: "One of the most beautiful features of the country is the Coeur d'Alene Lake, which is embosomed in the midst of gently sloping hills--the irregularity of its form, and the changing aspect of scenery about it, make it one of the most picturesque objects of the interior."

As the railroads and steamboats were built the tourists found Coeur d'Alene Lake, and the St. Joe and Coeur d'Alene Rivers favorite vacation and outing places. Camping, hunting, boating, and fishing were popular pastimes. Lodges, hotels and the transportation industry developed to accommodate the tourists. The Red Collar Steamship Line promoted the area with fancy brochures and special excursion rates.

Fred Murphy: "The steamboats come into vogue when there was no roads and no highways around the lakes. People would come in on the electric train. They would unload and get on those boats and go to St. Maries, Harrison and spots around the lake. Quite a few years later the automobile came in and they started building roads. Then people wanted to ride their automobiles instead of boats. God, if I had the old Georgie Oakes *today I could make a million dollars a year with it. Driving was a thrill in those days. Now it's work."*

The development of the automobile and the improvement of highways changed the way people came into the area and signaled the end of the steamboat era and the beginning of an era when people traveled independently. Lodges and gas stations were built along the roadsides to serve the needs of the automobile and the traveler.

Previous page: ***The Georgie Oakes, about 1910.*** The Red Collar Steamship Line offered excursions on the shadowy St. Joe River. The round trip from Coeur d'Alene to the head of navigation was 200 miles.
TrW-10-53

Ladies' cabin on the steamer Idaho. The large steamers on
Coeur d'Alene Lake provided plush accommodations for its
passengers. The Red Collar Steamship Line offered dining on
its Sunday excursions up the shadowy St. Joe River.
TrW-12-35

Loffs Bay, about 1910. This bay, located on the west side of
Lake Coeur d'Alene, was named after an early homesteader,
John Loff.
Rec-7-23

Boating on the Coeur d'Alene River, about 1910. Henry and Lillian
Rust with Mr. and Mrs. Brockman in their boat, the *O. U. Trout,*
poling up the Coeur d'Alene River in search of a camping spot.
Rec-7-25

Toad Rock, Mica Bay, about 1910.
LCD-15-4

Kid Island, about 1910. This Island, it is said, was named Kid Island by steamboat Captain Sorenson because his children and grandchildren enjoyed playing there.
LCD-13-3

Black Rock, about 1915. Lake Coeur d'Alene has many places to
explore by boat.
LCD-4-2

The Cash Store at Black Rock, 1907.
LCD-4-4

The Coeur d'Alene and Spokane electric line dock, about 1910.
The Coeur d'Alene and Spokane electric interurban railway was
built in 1903 by F. A. Blackwell and associates. Passengers could
connect with steamers in Coeur d'Alene and reach many desti-
nations around the lake. The line continued until the 1930s.
CDA-10-44

Blackwell Park. The park was built as part of the Coeur d'Alene and Spokane Railway. The fountain at the right center spouted water out at the top that was caught in the upper basin, then filtered down to keep the moss green. The lower basin held goldfish. The park, located around the terminal, was built by F. A. Blackwell to accommodate the tourists arriving in Coeur d'Alene on the railroad. This was just to the east of where Independence Point is today. *Rec-1-36*

Boating and fishing at Prichard Creek, in the Coeur d'Alene Mountains, about 1910.
Rec-3-59

Leaving Avery for the upper swift water of the St. Joe. The swift water is famous for its beautiful scenery and unsurpassed trout fishing. Pack horses were used to take gear into the rugged terrain of the St. Joe River country for hunting and fishing trips. *Rec-3-75*

Big cedar trees in the upper St. Joe River area, about 1910.
Hiking and camping were popular pastimes.
Rec-9-34

Hunting and fishing party. The Coeur d'Alene region has long been known as a paradise for hunters and fishermen. In 1908 a license cost one dollar.
Rec-3-28

Silver Tip Spokane Transportation Club outing on the St. Joe River, about 1910. The Coeur d'Alene Region was a popular destination point for people from Spokane.
Rec-3-112

Silver Tip Spokane Transportation Club outing on the St. Joe River, about 1910.
Rec-3-111

***Cataldo Mission, Mr. and Mrs. John Brockman and Mr. and Mrs.
Henry Rust, about 1910.*** The "Old Church", as it was known,
was completed in 1853. In 1877 new boundaries for the reservation were established and the church was not within those
boundaries. The Coeur d'Alene Tribe was moved to DeSmet.
The church became a favorite spot for visitors. Beginning in 1910
the Red Collar Steamship Line offered excursions up the Coeur
d'Alene River to the mission. Weekday rates from Spokane were
$4.00 and Sunday rates were $2.50, for the daylong trip.
Rel-2-40

Summer camp at the mouth of Slate Creek on the St. Joe River, about 1910. Judge and Mrs. Horace Hubbard at the table of their summer camp at the mouth of Slate Creek on the St. Joe River. They are camping while waiting for their house to be built at 603 N. Seventh in Coeur d'Alene.
Rec-3-105

Iva and John Brockman camping, about 1910. Here you can see the string to the camera in Mr. Brockman's hand. Hammocks were popular on camping trips.
Rec-3-54

Hotel Idaho. Built in 1903 this hotel cost $100,000. It had eighty rooms and was a popular resort for tourists. Located on the north side of Sherman Avenue between First and Second streets, it burned in 1972.
CDA-11-16

Dance Pavilion at Arrow Point, after 1892. Soldiers and band members from Fort Sherman enjoyed dances at the pavilion. Tree boughs provided the roof. Joseph Boughton built the pavilion in 1892. *LCD-1-5*

Coeur d'Alene City Beach, about 1920.
Rec-6-91

The Steamer Harrison at Harrison, about 1915. The dock is crowded with people under a banner that says "Our City Is Tours".
Har-2-27

Harvey Kelly and George Moyers boxing at the Harrison
Regatta, 7/4/1916.
Har-3-3

Steamer Georgie Oakes at Harrison, about 1920.
TrW-10-52

Boat house and the Colfax at Arrow Point, about 1910. House boating was very popular on Lake Coeur d'Alene as an inexpensive means of summer recreation.
LCD-1-2

Lake Chatcolet dedication, Aug. 16, 1925. In 1925 the lake was opened for navigation. Once known as "chat cak alye" (meaning "lake") by the Coeur d'Alene tribe, it has long been a favored spot for camping and fishing for both Indians and tourists. It was also famous for black bass.
LCht-1-1

Conkling Park, about 1915. Conkling Park was located just beyond Harrison and featured a main building, dining hall, dancing pavilion, a store and cottages. The park was reached from Spokane by the Inland Empire Express (electric line) to Coeur d'Alene, then a Red Collar steamer. Two steamers departed daily from the park.
LCD-8-7

Conkling Park, about 1913.
LCD-8-12

The writer of a 1916 pamphlet boasted about Conkling Park:
"Something is doing every hour of the day. Those who prefer a book,
or to write, or rest, have the lake shore, or woods, or their room, while
others choose tennis, or boating, bathing, planning some evening sur-
prise, or the like. The table is the best home cooking. Mrs. Conkling is
noted in this regard and endeavors to please."

St. Maries waterfront, about 1910. Steamer *Seattle* is at the dock.
St. Maries was a supply point for packers on their way to the St.
Joe country.
StM-2-3

St. Maries waterfront, about 1910. Steamer *Georgie Oakes* at dock.
Farmers and lumberjacks reached the St. Maries and St. Joe river
valleys by steamer. The fertile farming lands and what seemed
like limitless timber supplies attracted many settlers.
StM-2-4

St. Maries Hotel dining room, about 1910.
StM-4-1

The Lee's Lodge on the Fourth of July summit. The Mullan Tree and the Mullan Statue were located here when the Lees leased land from the Forest Service and built this gas station and the Summit Lodge in the mid 1920s. They had a trained bear and pet deer to entertain those who chose to stop after the climb up the pass.
MR-3-5

Ferrell Hotel on the St. Joe River, about 1910. Ferrell boasted that it was the highest mountain town on the highest navigable river in the world.
SJC-1-20

The Fish Inn. Built in 1932, the Fish Inn was designed to attract attention along the highway. Gas stations were located every few miles along the major highways. Kenneth and Marie West were inspired to build the inn in the shape of a fish after visitors brought in two fine bass. The Fish Inn burned down in 1996. *LCD-24-3*

REFERENCES

An Illustrated History of North Idaho, Embracing Nez Perce, Idaho, Latah, Kootenai and Shoshone Counties, State of Idaho. Chicago: Western Historical Publishing Company, 1903.

Anderson, Augusta. *The Shadowy St. Joe.* Spokane, Washington: Inland Printing Co. Scrapbook on file at the Museum of North Idaho.

Anderton, Peg Gott. *Early Schools In Idaho 1865-1960, Kootenai County, Bonner County, Boundary County and Benewah County.* Post Falls, Idaho: Self-published, 1986.

   Pleasantview, Kootenai County, Idaho: From 1858, South of the Spokane River, with Biographies, Post Falls School District 273 Consolidation. Post Falls, Idaho: Self-published, 1986.

   Green's Ferry and Cedar Creek School, Kootenai County, Idaho, from 1883. Post Falls, Idaho: Self-published, 1986.

Barnard, T. N. *Coeur d'Alene Towns and Mines, Mountains and Lakes.* Wallace, Idaho: Barnard Studios, ca. 1890.

Barton, David. *Idaho Panhandle Oral History Collection and Informant Transcripts: Idaho Panhandle National Forests Oral History Study.* Appendix B. Bloomington, Indiana: Soil Systems, Inc., 1980. On file at the Museum of North Idaho.

Boone, Lalia. *Idaho Place Names: A Geographical Dictionary.* Moscow, Idaho: University of Idaho Press, 1988.

Business Directory of Spokane and Neighboring Cities and Towns in Washington and Idaho. Spokane, Washington: Mercantile Directory Company & C.W. Hill Printing Co., 1910-1911.

Carbonneau Kincaid, Simone, Carl Ritchie & Diana Rigg. *Cultural Resource Inventory of the Monument West, Monument West Addition & Handspike Helicopter Timber Sales.* Archaeological surveys 79-24, 54, 55. Idaho Panhandle National Forest, 1980. On file at the U.S. Forest Service, Idaho Panhandle National Forest, Coeur d'Alene, Idaho.

Carbonneau Kincaid, Simone. *Cultural Resource Inventory of the Miller Can, Murray, and TE Break Timber Sales, Fernan Ranger District.* Idaho Panhandle National Forest, 1982.

Chamberlain, Barbara G. *North Idaho's Centennial, 1890-1990.* Coeur d'Alene, Idaho: Coeur d'Alene Press, 1990.

Coeur d'Alene, Idaho: Scenic City by the Unsalted Sea. Pamphlet of Red Collar Line, Coeur d'Alene and St. Joe Transportation Company, Ltd., Coeur d'Alene, Idaho: Press Publishing Company, 1905. On file at the Museum of North Idaho.

Coeur d'Alene Regional Scrapbook. On file (93.1.110) at the Museum of North Idaho.

Conley, Cort. *Idaho for the Curious: A Guide.* Cambridge, Idaho: Backeddy Press, 1982.

Crowell, Sandra A. & David O. Asleson. *Up the Swiftwater:* A Pictorial History of the Upper St. Joe Valley. Published by the authors, 1980. Revised edition: Coeur d'Alene, Idaho: Museum of North Idaho, 1995.

Dunnigan, Lorretta. *Early History of Coeur d'Alene.* Master's thesis on file at Gonzaga University, Spokane, Washington, ca. 1960.

Ellis, Mamie, et al. *The Way We Were: A History of Early Schools in Idaho.* Bicentennial project sponsored by the Idaho Falls Chapter of the Retired Teacher's Association, 1976.

Emerson, Tom. *Fred Murphy: A Legend of Coeur d'Alene Lake.* Coeur d'Alene, Idaho: Century Publishing Company, 1988.

Fahey, John. *Inland Empire: D. C. Corbin and Spokane.* Seattle, Washington: University of Washington Press, 1965 The Ballyhoo Bonanza: Charles Sweeny and the Idaho Mines. Seattle and London: University of Washington Press, 1971.

Grantham, A., ed. (secretary of Coeur d'Alene Chamber of Commerce). *Coeur d'Alene, the Gem City of the Gem State Idaho.* Coeur d'Alene, Idaho: Coeur d'Alene Press, 1934.

Hammes, Robert M. & E. Mark Justice, eds. *The Way It Was.* St. Maries, Idaho: Western Historical, Inc., 1962.

Harrison Searchlight. Newspaper published in Harrison, Idaho, 1953 and 1992 issues. On file at the Museum of North Idaho.

Hawley, James H., ed. *History of Idaho, Gem of the Mountains.* Vol. 1. Chicago: S. J. Clarke Publishing Company, 1920.

Hensley, Marianne. Personal communications and written sources, 1989-1991. On file at the Museum of North Idaho.

Holmes, F. W., ed. *Panhandle Magazine*, Vol. 1, No. 1. Coeur d'Alene, Idaho: Panhandle Publishing Co., May 1908.

Hudson, Lorelea, et al. *Cultural Resource Overview for the Colville and Idaho Panhandle National Forests and the Bureau of Land Management-Spokane and Coeur d'Alene Districts.* Vol. 1, Appendix 34. Sandpoint, Idaho: 1981.

Hult, Ruby El. *Steamboats in the Timber.* Caldwell, Idaho: Caxton Printers, 1952.

Koch, Maxine (Hoag). *Adventure into the Past* (A History of Worley, Idaho). Self-published, 1989. On file at the Museum of North Idaho.

Magnuson, Richard G. *Coeur d'Alene Diary: the First Ten Years of Hardrock Mining in North Idaho.* Portland, Oregon: Metropolitan Press, 1968.

Manring, B. F. *Conquest of the Coeur d'Alenes and Palouses.* Spokane, Washington: John W. Graham & Company, 1912.

Miller, Don, & Stan Cohen. *The Big Burn: The Northwest's Great Forest Fire of 1910.* Missoula, Montana: Pictorial Histories Publishing Company, 1978.

Mullan, Captain John. *Miner's and Traveller's Guide.* New York: W. M. Franklin, 1865. Reprinted by Ye Galleon Press, Fairfield, Washington, 1991.

Museum of North Idaho Photograph Collection. On file at the Museum of North Idaho.

Museum of North Idaho Archives. On file at the Museum of North Idaho.

Montgomery, James. *Liberated Woman: A Life of May Arkwright Hutton.* Fairfield, Washington: Ye Galleon Press, 1974.

Official Handbook of the Coeur d'Alene Mines, Idaho Territory, and Needham Family Memoirs (by Gordon Needham). Reprinted by Ye Galleon Press, Fairfield, Washington, 1988. *Official Handbook* was originally printed by Lewis & Dryden, Portland, Oregon, 1884.

Osterberg, David. *Historical Reference Guide to Kootenai County, Idaho.* Published in cooperation with the Kootenai County Free Library District and Panhandle Regional Library System, Coeur d'Alene, Idaho, 1983.

Panhandle of Idaho. Coeur d'Alene, Idaho: Coeur d'Alene Commercial Club, 1909. Pamphlet on file at the Museum of North Idaho.

Peacock, M.D., Eldred G. "Early Idaho Panhandle Doctor Reached Patients on Horsebacks, Boats and Rails," *Pacific Northwestern*, Winter 1979, Vol. 23, No. 1. Pamphlet on file at the Museum of North Idaho.

Peltier, Jerome. *A Brief History of the Coeur d'Alene Indians, 1806-1909.* Fairfield, Washington: Ye Galleon Press, 1981.

    Antoine Plante: Mountain Man, Rancher, Hostler and Ferryman. Fairfield, Washington: Ye Galleon Press, 1983.

Plain Facts for the Homeseeker About Coeur d'Alene and Kootenai County, Idaho. Pamphlet on file at the Museum of North Idaho. Coeur d'Alene, Idaho, ca. 1915.

Polk, R. L. *Kootenai County Directories*. Spokane, Washington: R.L. Polk & Company, 1911-1990.

Renk, Nancy F. "Back to Basics: The Lake Pend Oreille Lime and Cement Industry and Its Regional Impact", *Idaho Yesterdays: Journal of Idaho and Northwest History*, Vol. 36, No. 1, Spring 1992, p. 211.

Russell, Bert. *Calked Boots*. Harrison, Idaho: Lacon Publishers, 1967.
        Hardships and Happy Times. Harrison, Idaho: Lacon Publishers, 1978.
        Swiftwater People. Harrison, Idaho: Lacon Publishers, 1979. Museum of North Idaho.
        North Fork of the Coeur d'Alene River. Harrison, Idaho: Lacon Publishers, 1984. Museum of North Idaho.

Sayler, Kathleen, et al. *Reflections From North Idaho: Vikings' View of the Centennial*. By the students of K. Sayler's English classes at Coeur d'Alene High School, 1990. On file at the Museum of North Idaho.

Smith, Esther Pond. *Excelsior Beach on Lower Twin Lake, Kootenai County, Idaho*. Self-published, 1966. On file at the Museum of North Idaho.

Souvenir of Coeur d'Alene, Idaho. Coeur d'Alene, Idaho: Berry and Saunders Stationers, ca. 1900. On file at the Museum of North Idaho.

Straffin, Fred, et al. *Souvenir of St. Maries, Idaho*. St. Maries, Idaho: Western Photo and Publishing Company. 1911. Pamphlet on file at the Museum of North Idaho.

Strong Clarence & Clyde S. Webb. *White Pine: King of Many Waters*. Missoula, Montana: Mountain Press Publishing Company, 1970.

Teit, James, in Franz Boas, ed. *Coeur d'Alene, Flathead and Okanogan Indians*, 45th Annual Report of Bureau of American Ethnology, 1927-1928. Washington: U.S. Government Printing Office, 1930. Reprinted by Ye Galleon Press, Fairfield, Washington, 1985.

Toth, B. E. *Trek to America: A Story of an Immigrant Hungarian Family in the United States*. Self-published. On file at the Museum of North Idaho.

Walker Jr., Deward. *Indians of Idaho*. Moscow, Idaho: University of Idaho Press, 1978.

Weeks, George F. *Coeur d'Alene: Beautiful and Progressive*. Coeur d'Alene, Idaho, 1924. Pamphlet on file at the Museum of North Idaho.

White, J. C. (mgr. of the Red Collar Line). *Lake and River Excursions via Red Collar S.S. Line in the Panhandle of Idaho, Vacations in Idaho in Beautiful Lake Coeur d'Alene, Shadowy St. Joe River, Coeur d'Alene River and Lakes*. Spokane, Washington: C.E. Flagg, 1911. Pamphlet on file at the Museum of North Idaho.

Wilhelm, Patti, ed. *History of the Churches of the Northern Deanery of the Diocese of Boise*. Roman Catholic Diocese of Boise, Idaho, 1990.

Wilkins, Clement. "Backward Glances", *Kootenai County Leader*, Coeur d'Alene, Idaho, ca. 1950s.

Wood, John V. *Railroads Through the Coeur d'Alenes*. Caldwell, Idaho: Caxton Printers Ltd., 1983.

INDEX